Base SAS

Interview Questions
You'll Most Likely Be Asked

Job Interview Questions Series

VP **Vibrant Publishers**
www.vibrantpublishers.com

Base SAS Interview Questions
You'll Most Likely Be Asked

© 2012, By Vibrant Publishers, USA. All rights reserved. No part of this publication may be reproduced or distributed in any form or by any means, or stored in a database or retrieval system, without the prior permission of the publisher.

ISBN-10: 1475188331
ISBN-13: 9781475188332

Library of Congress Control Number: 2012906684

This publication is designed to provide accurate and authoritative information in regard to the subject matter covered. The author has made every effort in the preparation of this book to ensure the accuracy of the information. However, information in this book is sold without warranty either expressed or implied. The Author or the Publisher will not be liable for any damages caused or alleged to be caused either directly or indirectly by this book.

Vibrant Publishers books are available at special quantity discount for sales promotions, or for use in corporate training programs. For more information please write to **bulkorders@vibrantpublishers.com**

Please email feedback / corrections (technical, grammatical or spelling) to **spellerrors@vibrantpublishers.com**

To access the complete catalogue of Vibrant Publishers, visit
www.vibrantpublishers.com

Table of Contents

1.	Basics	7
2.	Referencing Files	11
3.	SAS Programs	17
4.	Reports - List and Summary	21
5.	SAS Data Sets	27
6.	Data Step	33
7.	Formats	37
8.	Statistics	41
9.	Outputs	49
10.	Variables	53
11.	Combining Data Sets	59
12.	SAS Functions	67
13.	DO Loops	81
14.	Arrays	89
15.	Raw Data	95
16.	Date and Time Value	111
17.	Line Pointer Controls	117
18.	HR Questions	133
INDEX		155

This page is intentionally left blank

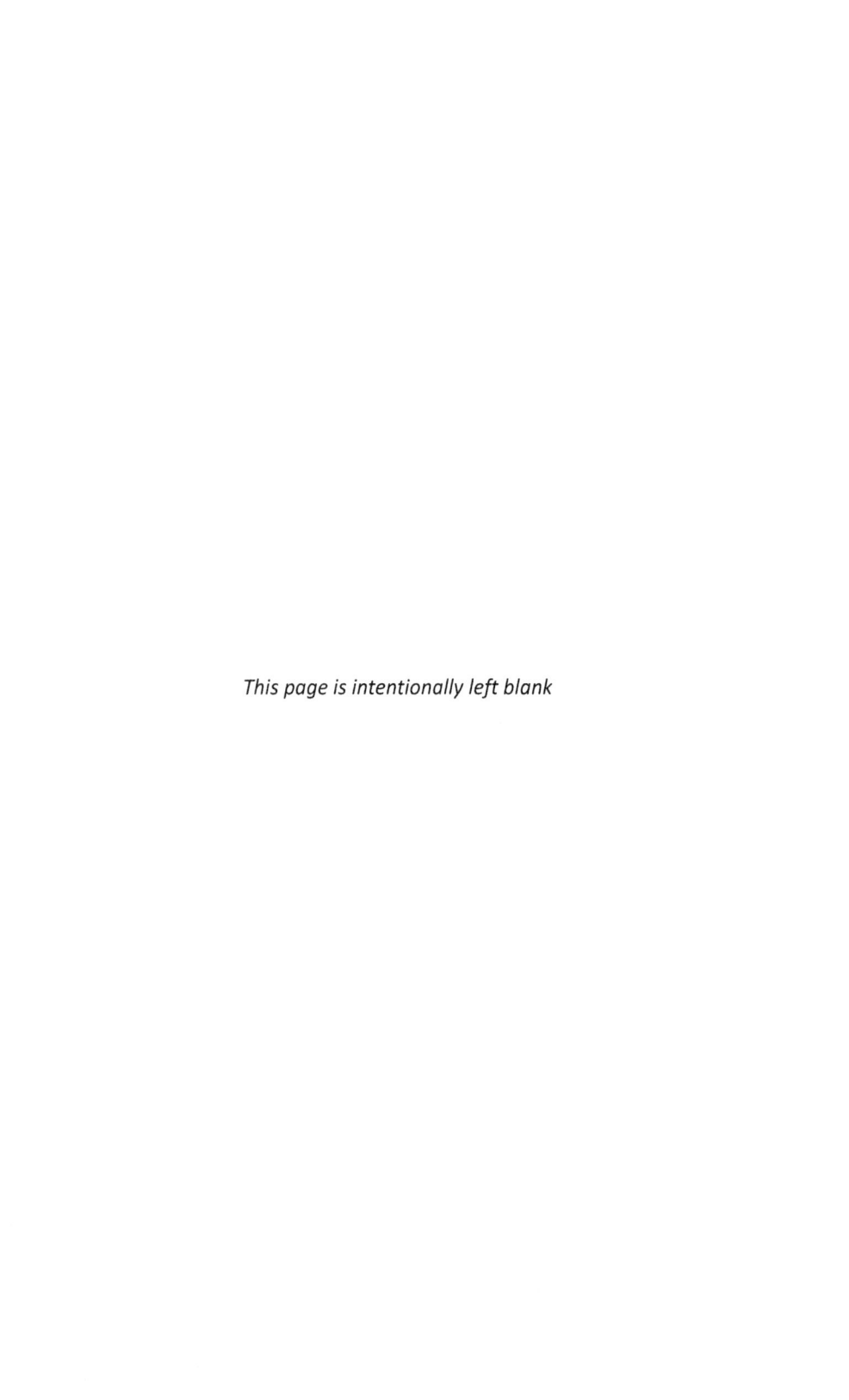

Base SAS Interview Questions

Review these typical interview questions and think about how you would answer them. Read the answers listed; you will find best possible answers along with strategies and suggestions.

This page is intentionally left blank

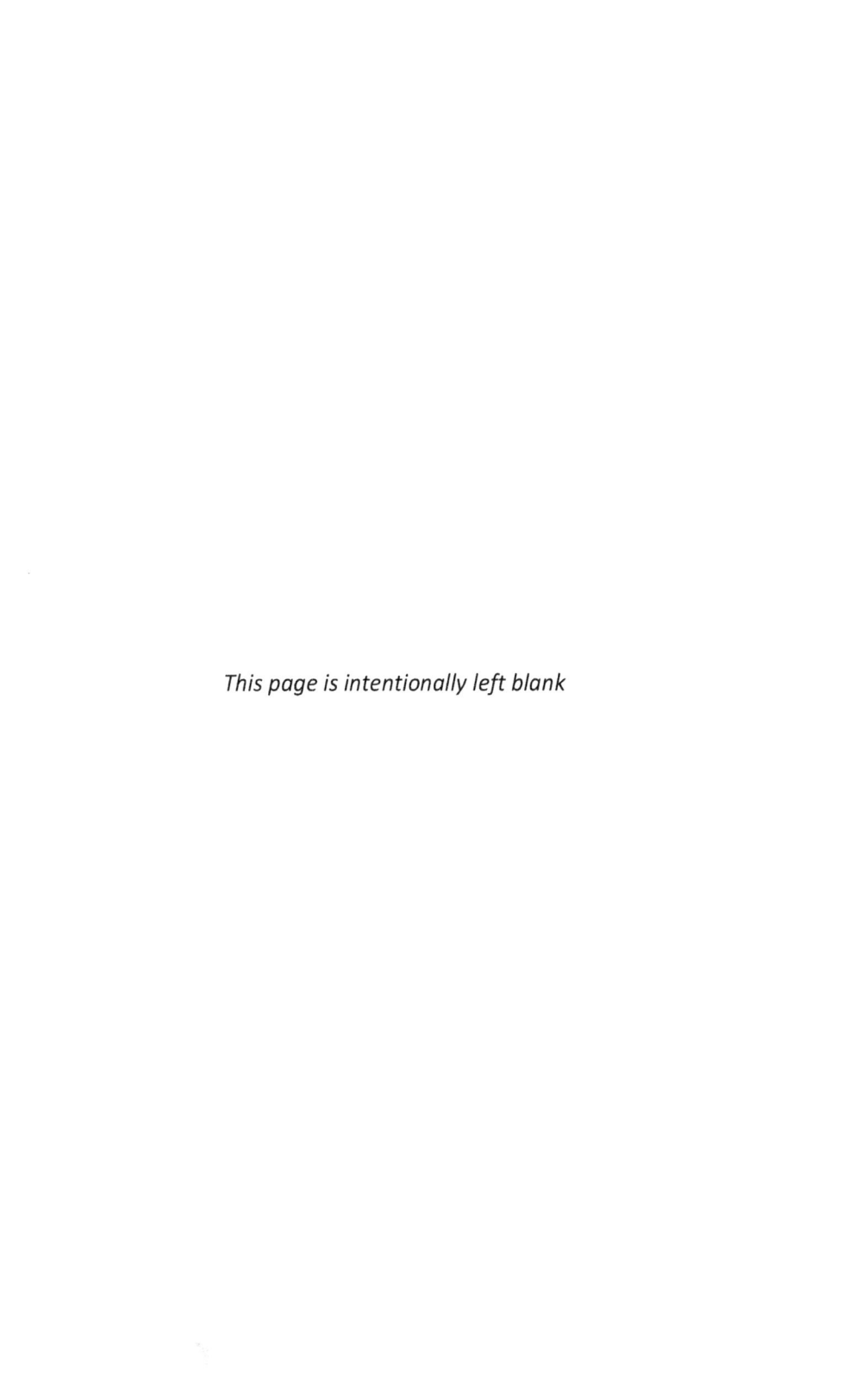

Basics

1: You might be already familiar with the dataset. What is the descriptor portion of the data set?
Answer:
Descriptor portion of the data set contains information about the data set like name of the data set, date and time when it was created, number of observation, number of variables and attribute information for each variable in the dataset.

2: Which parameters describe a variable in SAS?
Answer:
A variable can be best described by name, type, length, format, informat and label in SAS.

3: How does SAS recognise the end of a step and execute the previous step?
Answer:
Whenever SAS encounters a Data, PROC, Run or Quit statement, SAS executes the previous step.

4: How do we reference a permanent SAS data set?
Answer:
A permanent SAS data set can be referenced by a two level name- 'libref.filename'. libref is the name of the library to which SAS file belongs and filename is the name of the data set. A period separates both libref and filename. E.g.: To reference a SAS data set named questionset1 which is stored in the library exam, we use the two level name -exam.questionset1.

5: What is the default length of numeric variables?
Answer:
Numeric variables are stored as floating point numbers in 8 bytes of storage unless we specify different length. The default length of numeric variables is 8.

This page is intentionally left blank

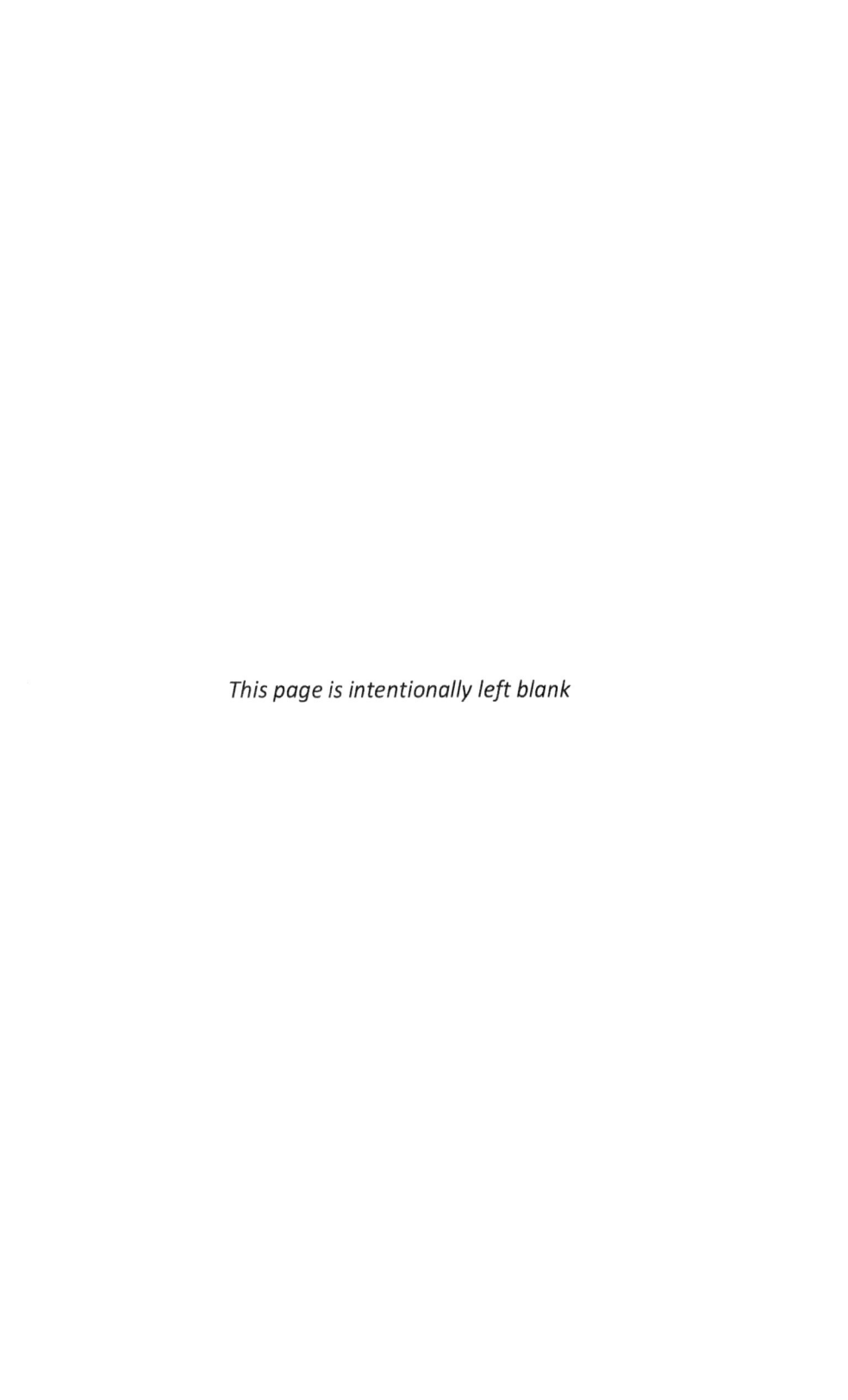

Referencing Files

6: How do you verify after assigning a libref?
Answer:
When a libname statement is submitted, a message is displayed in log window stating that libref has been successfully assigned. Thus checking the log window enables us to verify the libref.

7: What is the purpose of a SAS engine?
Answer:
SAS engine is the set of internal instructions which SAS uses for writing to and reading from files in the SAS library. SAS can read or write files by using appropriate engine for that file type.

8: Describe some ways to view the contents of SAS data set.
Answer:
There are three ways for viewing the contents of a SAS data set - Proc contents, Proc data sets and opening the libraries folder in the explored window.
Eg : To view the contents of a dataset 'questionset2' stored in the library 'exam' the following programs can be used.
proc contents data=exam.questionset2;
run;

OR

proc datasets;
contents data=exam.questionset2;

quit;

9: Which option is used to list the variables in creation order or order of logical position while viewing the dataset with proc contents?

Answer:

VARNUM OPTION can be used for listing the variables in logical order. By default PROC CONTENTS and PROC DATASETS list variables alphabetically. Specifying varnum option causes the variables to be listed in the order of logical position.

The following example illustrates the use of varnum option with proc contents. varnum option causes the variables in the data set questionset2 to be listed in the creation order.

proc contents data=exam.questionset2 varnum;
run;

10: How do you modify SAS system options like page number, time etc?

Answer:

OPTIONS STATEMENT can be submitted to modify system options.

In the following example an OPTIONS statement is submitted to change the following options- date and pageno. Since the option is set to nodate, SAS displays no date in the output. Also in the output, the numbering of the page starts from 3 since pageno option is set to 3.

options nodate pageno=3;

proc contents data=exam.questionset2 varnum;
run;

11: How SAS handles two digit year values?
Answer:
When SAS reads two digit year values it is interpreted based on 100 year span which starts with YEARCUTOFF= value. The default value of YEARCUTOFF = is 1920.

It is possible to override the default value and change the value of YEARCUTOFF= to the first year of another 100 year span.

12: Suppose your dataset exam.questionset2 contains 20 observations. How do you print only the last 11 observations?
Answer:
This can be achieved by using FIRSTOBS=10 option. SAS reads tenth observation first and then reads till the last observation.
E.g.:
options firstobs=10;
proc print data=exam.questionset2;
run;

13: Suppose your dataset exam.questionset2 contains 20 observations. How do you print the observations from 12-17?
Answer:
This can be achieved by combining FIRSTOBS= and OBS= option.
E.g.:
options firstobs= 12 obs= 17;

proc print data=exam.questionset2;
run;

14: Describe the SOURCE system option used in SAS?
Answer:
The SOURCE system option controls whether SAS source statements are to be written to SAS log. The default system setting is SOURCE.
The syntax is SOURCE | NOSOURCE.
SOURCE - specifies to write SAS SOURCE statements to SAS log.
NOSOURCE - specifies not to write SAS SOURCE statements to SAS log.

15: Describe the REPLACE option in detail.
Answer:
This specifies that the permanently stored data sets can be replaced. If the option NOREPLACE is used the inadvertent replacing of existing datasets can be prevented.
The syntax is REPLACE | NOREPLACE.
REPLACE - specifies that a permanently stored data set can be replaced with another data set of same name.
NOREPLACE - specifies that a permanently stored data set cannot be replaced with another data set of same name. This helps in preventing replacing data sets by mistake

This page is intentionally left blank

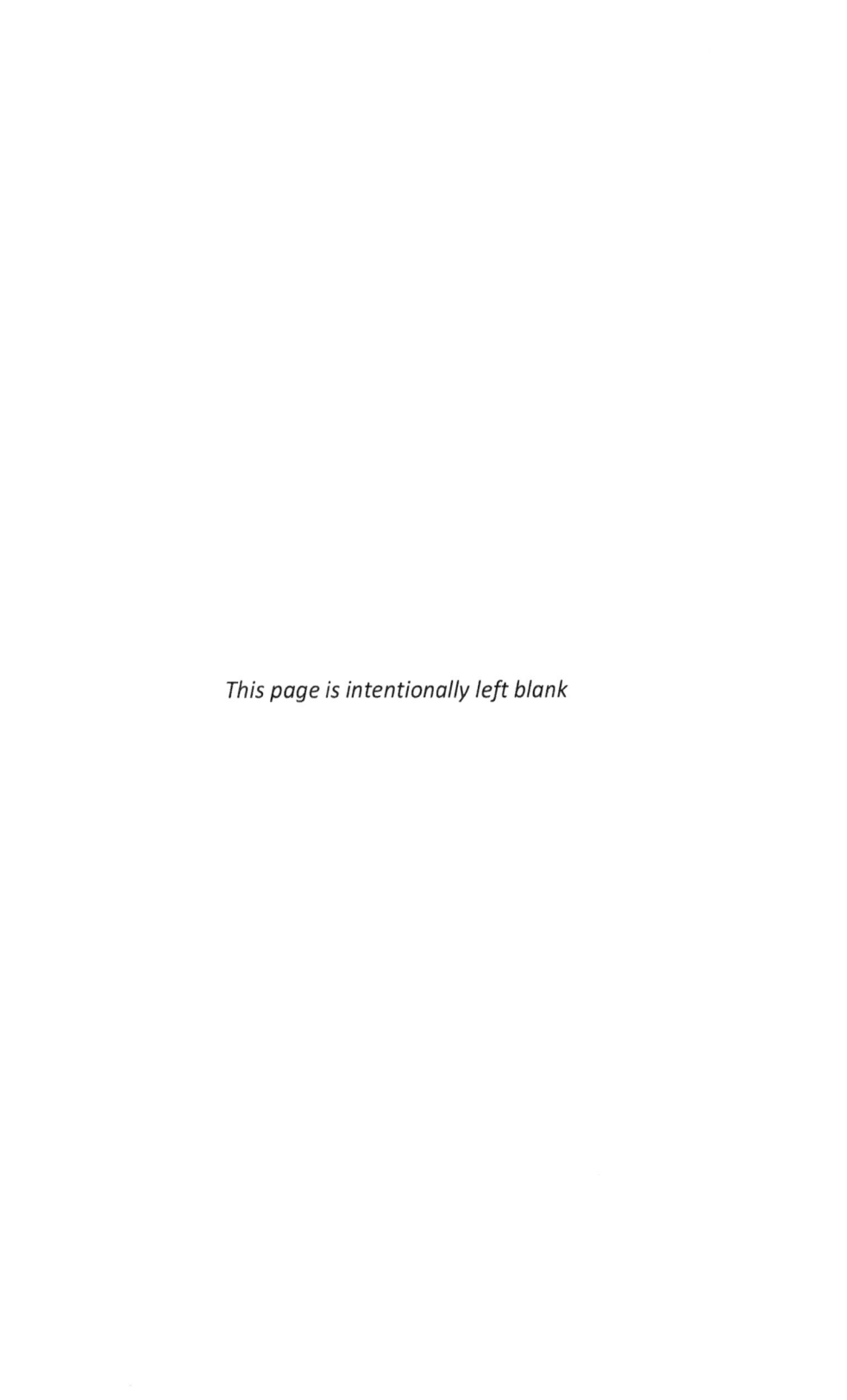

SAS Programs

16: What is the function of INCLUDE command in SAS?
Answer:
The INCLUDE command includes/opens a stored program in the Windows operating environment. Using include command enables us to open a stored program in the code editing window. As this is a command there is no need to add semi-colon at the end.
Suppose you want to include the program set2.sas which is stored in d:\sas you can issue the following command:
include 'd:\sas\set2.sas'

17: What are the two categories of error commonly encountered in SAS?
Answer:
The two types of errors are data error and syntax errors. Syntax errors occur when the programming statements do not comply with the rules of the language. Data errors are those errors which occur when some data values are not suitable for the SAS statements mentioned.
E.g.:
Syntax error - One common example of a syntax error is missing a semi-colon at the end of a SAS statement. In the following example, semi-colon is missing in the print statement which illustrates syntax error.
proc print data = exam.questionset2
run;

Data Error - One common example of data error is assigning a character value to a numeric variable.

18: Suppose after submitting a SAS program you see the statement 'Data step running' at the top of active window. What does that indicate and how do you resolve the issue?
Answer:
This indicates that there is a syntax error. The error is that the data step which is submitted does not have a run statement. So the data step does not execute and hence this message appears on the top of active window.

This can be resolved by submitting a run statement to complete the data step.

19: How do you specify comments in SAS?
Answer:
There are two ways of specifying comment statements –
* this is a comment;
Or
/* this is another comment*/

20: How do you invoke the debugger in SAS?
Answer:
The debugger can be invoked by adding debug option in data statement and then executing the program.
E.g.:
data exam.questionset2 / debug;
infile exam;
input one $ two $;

run;

proc print data=exam.questionset2;

run;

Reports - List and Summary

21: How do you select the variables and control the order in which they appear while creating a list report?
Answer:
This can be achieved by using VAR statement in proc print.
E.g.:
proc print data=exam.questionset2;
var slno quest1 quest2 quest3;
run;

22: How to remove the column containing observation number while creating a list report?
Answer:
Using NOOBS option in the proc print statement enables us to remove the column containing observation number while creating list report.
E.g.:
proc print data=exam.questionset2 noobs;
var slno quest1 quest2 quest3;
run;

23: What is the output of proc print?
Answer:
proc print produces a report containing a column for observation number on the left, displays all the observations and variables in the dataset, variables in the order in which they appear in the data set.

24: How do you cancel a title statement?

Answer:

All the previous title statements can be cancelled by issuing a null title statement or submit a title1 statement with no text.

E.g.:

title1;

proc print data=exam.questionset2 noobs;

var slno quest1 quest2 quest3;

run;

The null title1 statement causes the cancellation of all the titles which were previously defined before the execution of proc print.

25: Suppose you are having a data set exam.questionset2. The data set contains a column date. You have to assign a format (mmddyy8.) temporarily to the date column so that it appears in the formatted way in the output. How do you do that?

Answer:

This can be achieved by using the format statement. format statement is applicable only to the proc step in which it appears.

Eg:

title1;

proc print data = exam.questionset2 noobs;

var slno quest1 quest2 quest3 date;

format date mmddyy8.;

run;

26: How do you assign a permanent label in SAS?

Answer:

A permanent label can be assigned by using the label statement in data step.

E.g.: The following program creates a data set exam.questionset3. Here the label statement is mentioned in the data step. So the label for the variable date is permanently assigned.

data exam.questionset3;

   set exam.questionset2;

   label date='Finish Date';

run;

proc print data = exam.questionset3 noobs;

run;

27: While creating a list report with proc report how do you select the variables and order them?

Answer:

This is achieved using column statement. column statement decides the order of variables while using proc report.

E.g.:

proc report data = exam.questionset2 ;

column slno quest1 quest2 quest3 date;

run;

28: Which option is used with proc report statement to underline all column headings and space between them?

Answer:

HEADLINE option can be used along with proc report for

underlining all the column headings and space between them.
E.g.:
proc report data = exam.questionset2 headline;
column slno quest1 quest2 quest3 date;
run;

29: What is the purpose of using order option in the define statement while using proc report?

Answer:

While using proc report, defining a variable as an order variable produces a list report with the rows ordered according to the formatted values. Proc report displays only the first occurrence of each value of an order variable in a set of rows which has same value for all order variables.

The following examples produce a report from the data set exam.questionset2. define statement used below defines set as order variable with label 'questionsetno' and width of 6.So the report contains rows ordered by the variable set.

proc report data=exam.questionset2 headline;
column set quest1 quest2 quest3 date;
define set/ order 'questionsetno' width=6;
run;

30: Which variables are used to calculate statistics in proc report?

Answer:

Analysis variables are used to produce statistics in proc report. By default all numeric variables are considered as analysis variables and used for the calculation of default statistics- sum.

SAS Data Sets

31: What is the function of infile statement?
Answer:
infile statement is used to indicate the external file in which the required data resides.

E.g:
infile ' D:\sas\programs\questionset1.dat' ;

32: Which is the ideal situation for using column input?
Answer:
Column input is used when data is:
   a) standard numeric or character values. Standard numeric data can only contain numbers, decimal points, numbers in scientific notation and plus or minus signs.
   b) in fixed columns. For each row the values for particular field begin and end in same columns.

33: How do you read the data lines entered directly into the program?
Answer:
DATALINES statement can be used as a last statement in the data step to read the data lines directly.

E.g.:
data exam.questionset3;
infile questfile;
input slno 1-4 author $ 5-12;
datalines;
This set contains formatted questions by famous authors
;

run;

34: What is the purpose of using the keyword _NULL_ in the data statement?
Answer:
NULL statement enables us to use the data step without creating a dataset.

The following example uses the keyword _NULL_ to use the data step without creating a dataset. The following example uses the keyword _NULL_ to create a raw data file by reading from the dataset 'exam.questionset1'. FILE statement specifies the output file location. PUT statement describes the lines to be written to the raw data file.

data _null_;
set exam.questionset1;
file 'd:\sas\set1.dat';
put setno 1-4 answers 5-25;
run;

35: What is the purpose of PUT statement?
Answer:
The PUT statement is used to describe the data to be written to a raw data file. It is analogous to the use of input statement while reading from a raw data file.

The following example illustrates the use of PUT statement to write to a raw data file referenced by the fileref 'questfile'.

data _null_;
set exam.questionset2;

file questfile;
put slno 1-4 author 5-12;
run;

36: Which parameters are to be mentioned in the input statement while using column input?
Answer:
While using column input the input statement should contain:
- a) SAS variable name
- b) Type ('$' sign if it is a character column)
- c) Starting column
- d) Ending column if necessary

E.g.:
data exam.questionset3;
infile questfile;
input slno 1-4 author $ 5-12;
run;

37: Usage of programming statement is one common way of creating a SAS dataset from raw data file. What is the other way of creating SAS dataset from a raw data file?
Answer:
SAS IMPORT WIZARD is an alternate way of creating a SAS dataset from different types of raw data files like Excel spreadsheets and text files.

38: What is the scope of a FILENAME statement?
Answer:

FILENAME statement is global. This means that the filename statement remains in effect until you modify it, cancel it or end the SAS session.

39: What is the significance of SET statement in SAS?
Answer:
SET statement specifies the data set from which the data is to be read.
E.g.: The following program creates a data set exam.questionset3 by reading the data from the data set exam.questionset2.
data exam.questionset3;
    set exam.questionset2;
    label date='Finish Date';
run;

40: Is it possible to use date constants to assign dates in ASSIGNMENT statements?
Answer:
Yes, it is possible to assign date constants.
E.g.: In the following program an assignment statement is used to assign a date constant to the variable testdate.
data exam.questionset3;
    set exam.questionset2;
    input slno 1-3 author $ 4-12;
    testdate='20MAR2012'd;
run;

This page is intentionally left blank

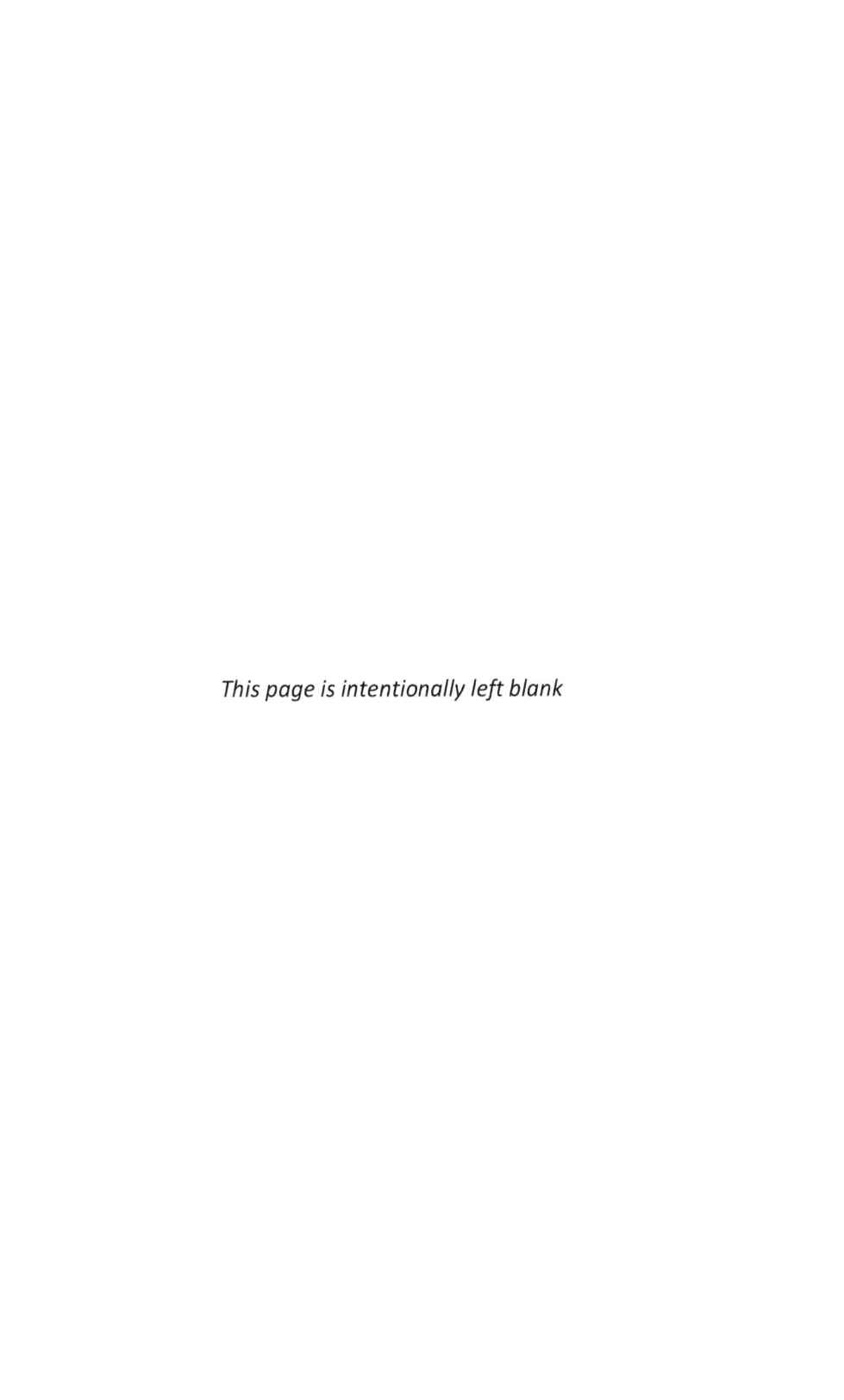

Data Step

41: Explain the compilation phase of data step in detail.
Answer:
During the compilation phase, the statements are scanned for syntax errors. If any syntax error is detected, further processing of data step is stopped. When compilation phase is complete, descriptor portion of new data set is created.

42: When is an input buffer created?
Answer:
Input buffer is an area of memory created to hold record from external file. Input buffer is created at the beginning of the compilation phase. It is created only when the raw data is read.

43: Explain the automatic variable _ERROR_.
Answer:
ERROR is an automatic variable in program data vector. This is used to specify the error caused by data during execution. The default value is zero. This variable is not written to data set.
E.g.: When the following simple program is submitted, SAS processes the data step. In the compilation phase a program data vector (pdv) is created to hold observations one at a time. This pdv contains two automatic variables - _N_ and _ERROR_. Also a slot is added to the pdv for each variable in the data set. At the end of compilation phase, descriptor portion is created but _N_ and _ERROR_ are not written to data set.
data exam.questionset3;

        infile exam;

        input slno 1-3 author $ 4-12;

run;

At the beginning of execution _ERROR_ is set to zero. If there is any error during execution, like a character value being assigned to a numeric variable, the variable _ERROR_ changes to 1, indicating that an error has occurred.

44: Explain the significance of _N_.
Answer:

_N_ is an automatic variable of program data vector which specifies the number of times the data step begins to execute. E.g.: When the following simple program is submitted, SAS processes the data step. In the compilation phase a program data vector (pdv) is created to hold observations one at a time. This pdv contains two automatic variables - _N_ and _ERROR_. Also a slot is added to the pdv for each variable in the data set. At the end of compilation phase descriptor portion is created but _N_ and _ERROR_ are not written to data set.

data exam.questionset3;

        infile exam;

        input slno 1-3 author $ 4-12;

run;

In the above example, SAS reads values from the file exam. Imagine the file 'exam' contains 9 records. Data step iterates 9 times as there are 9 records in the file. During the execution all the variables are read from file, stored in the pdv and written to the data set. In this case the data step executes 9 times. While reading first observation the value of _N_ is set to 1, for next observation _N_ is set to 2 and so on.

45: How do you limit the number of observations that are read during the data step?

Answer:

OBS= option can be used in the infile statement to limit the number of observations that are read during the data step.
E.g.: The following program creates a new data set exam.questionset3 with all the variables but only 10 observations as we used the option OBS=10.

data exam.questionset3 obs=10;
    infile exam;
    input slno 1-3 author $ 4-12;
run;

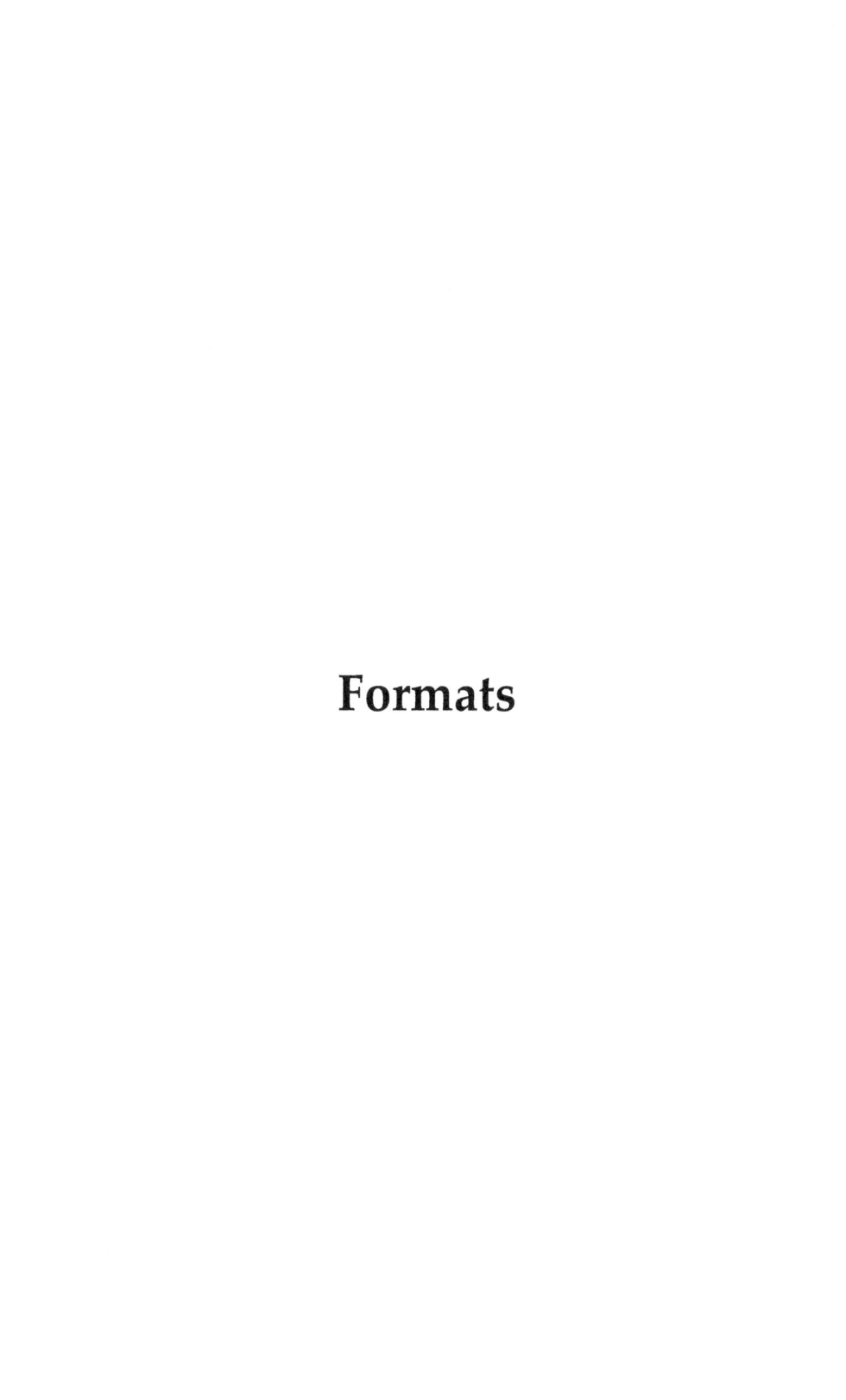

Formats

46: What is the maximum length of label?
Answer:
The label in SAS can be 256 characters long.

47: Explain the function of the keyword FMTLIB.
Answer:
FMTLIB displays the formats and values that are currently stored in the catalog.

48: How is VALUE statement used to create formats?
Answer:
VALUE statement is used to define formats for variables in the data set.
E.g.: The following program creates a format - questfmt. The value statement creates a format questfmt to assign the descriptive labels.

Proc format lib=library;
    value questfmt
    1-100='initial';
    101-200='middle';
    201-300='final';
run;

49: Which keyword is used in the value statement to label the missing value?
Answer:
The keyword OTHER is used in the value statement to label the missing values as well as unknown values.

E.g.: The following program creates a format - questfmt. The value statement creates a format questfmt to assign the descriptive labels. The values which do not fall in the range 1-300 as well as missing/unknown values are labelled using the keyword OTHER.

Proc format lib=library;
    value questfmt
    1-100='initial';
    101-200='middle';
    201-300='final'
other='unknown';
run;

This page is intentionally left blank

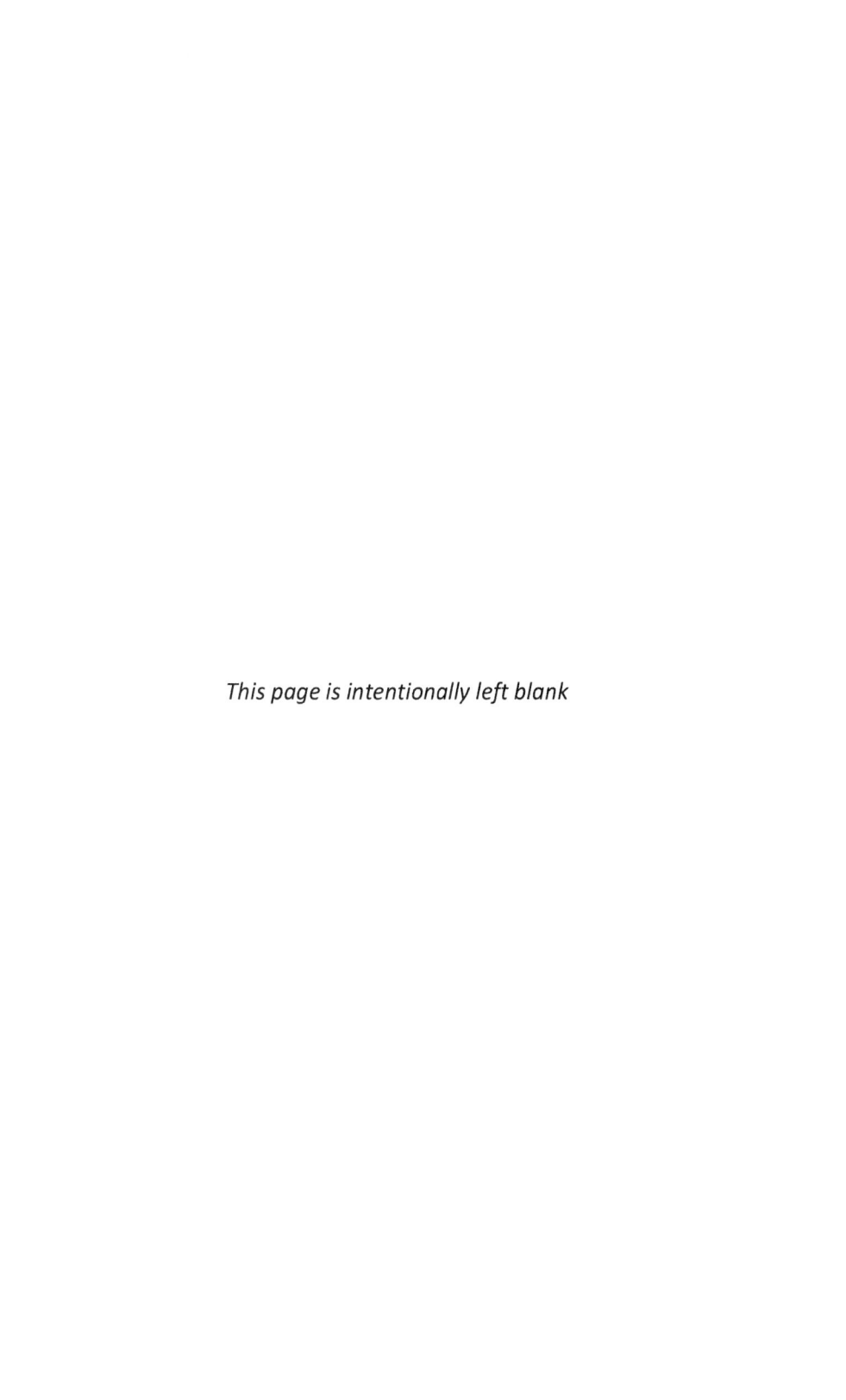

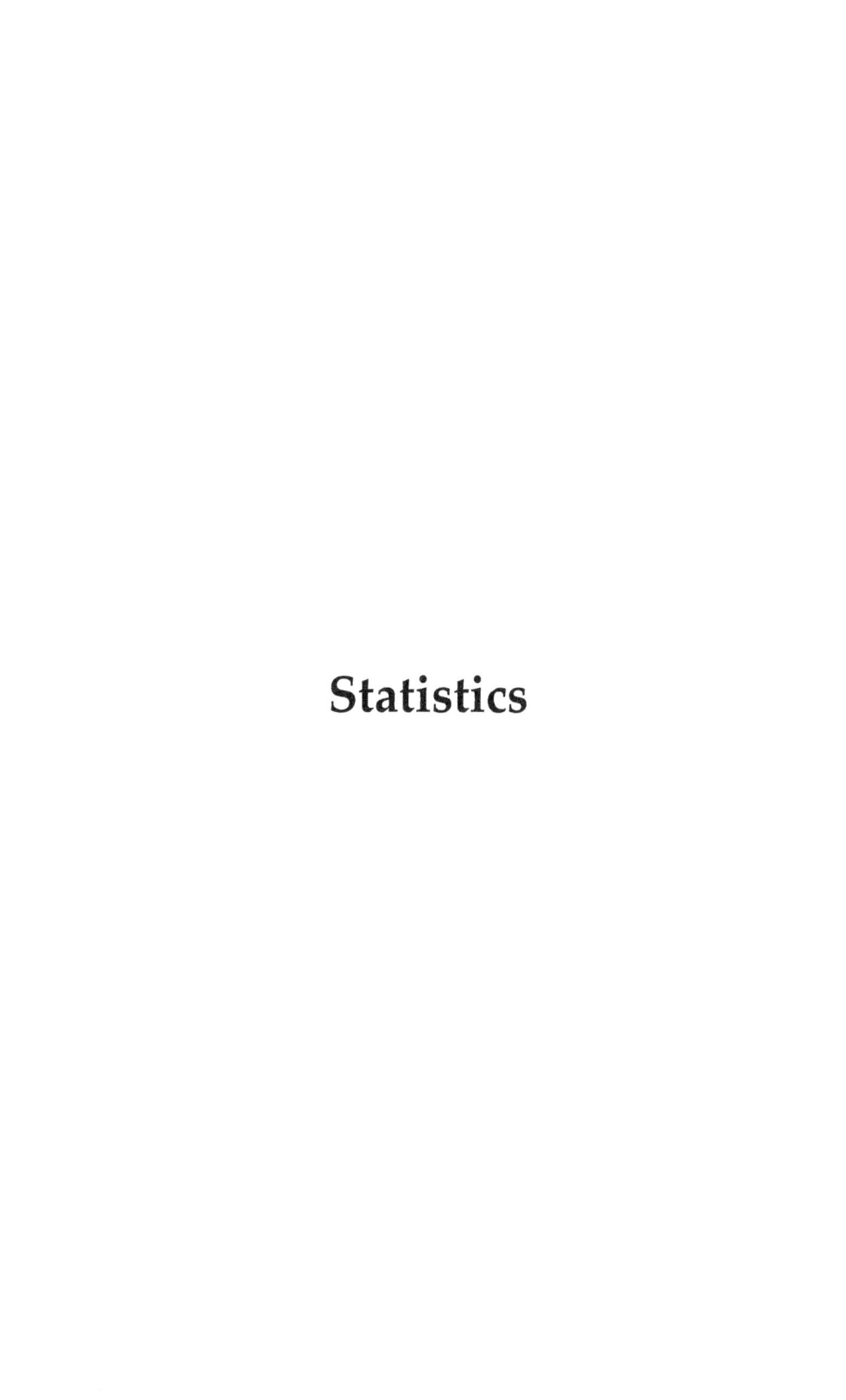

Statistics

50: Which is the ideal procedure to use for calculating the statistics for continuous numeric variables?

Answer:

PROC MEANS or PROC SUMMARY are ideal for calculating the statistics of numeric variables. Continuous numeric variables are those variables which are not discrete. E.g.: age of people.

The following procedure creates a report from the data set result with default statistics (n count, mean, standard deviation, minimum and maximum values) calculated for all numeric variables.

proc means data = exam.result;
run;

51: What are the default statistics produced by the MEANS procedure?

Answer:

MEANS procedure in its simplest form produces number of missing values, mean, standard deviation, minimum and maximum values of all numeric variables in the data set.

52: Suppose you had a dataset exam.set1 for which you wish to calculate the median of all numeric variables. How do you use the programming statements?

Answer:

This can be achieved by using MEANS procedure with the keyword MEDIAN.

E.g.:

proc means data= exam.set1 median;
run;

53: Which option is used in the PROC MEANS statement to limit the number of decimal places?

Answer:

MAXDEC= option is used to limit the number of decimal places in MEANS procedure.

E.g.: In the following program the option MAXDEC is set to 1. So, all the numeric variables will be having one decimal place in the report.

proc means data= exam.set1 maxdec=1;
run;

54: How do you specify variables in PROC MEANS statement?

Answer:

VAR statement can be used with PROC MEANS statement to exclude certain variables and produce statistics for the desired variables.

E.g.: In the following program the var statement is used to include three variables - marks1, marks2, marks5. PROC MEANS produces statistics for only these variables.

proc means data= exam.set1 maxdec=1;
var marks1 marks2 marks 5;
run;

55: Which statistics are generated for class variables in

MEANS procedure?

Answer:

There are no statistics generated for class variables by PROC MEANS. The values of class variables are used for classification of data. The class variables usually contain discrete values which can be used for grouping the data.

56: How can you prevent the default report creation in PROC MEANS?

Answer:

PROC MEANS produces a report by default and this can be prevented by using the option NOPRINT.

E.g.:

proc means data= exam.set1 noprint;

var markset1 markset2 markset3;

run;

57: What is the default output produced by PROC FREQ?

Answer:

In its simplest form PROC FREQ creates a one way table with frequency, percent, cumulative frequency, cumulative percent of each value of all the variables in the data set.

58: How do you specify variables to be processed by PROC FREQ?

Answer:

TABLES statement specifies the variables to be processed by PROC FREQ.

E.g.: In the following program TABLES statement specifies the number of variables and the order in which the variables are displayed.

proc freq data= exam.set1 ;
tables month setnumber;
run;

59: Explain the significance of NOCUM option.
Answer:
NOCUM option is usually added to the TABLES statement to prevent the display of cumulative frequency as well as cumulative percentage in one-way frequency table.

E.g.: The addition of NOCUM option to the TABLES statement in the following program causes the frequency and percent alone to be displayed in the output.

proc freq data= exam.set1 ;
tables month set / nocum;
run;

60: What are the criteria for the data to be used for BY group processing?
Answer:
Data must be sorted before using BY group processing. So it is necessary to run the PROC SORT before using PROC MEANS with BY statement.

61: What is the difference between the default output produced by PROC MEANS and PROC SUMMARY?

Answer:
The results which are produced by PROC MEANS and PROC SUMMARY are same. But the default output produced is different. PROC MEANS produces a report by default while PROC SUMMARY produces an output data set by default.

62: What are the default values produced when PROC FREQ is used for producing crosstabulations?
Answer:
The output table produced by crosstabulation have cell frequency, cell percentage of total frequency, cell percentage of row frequency and cell percentage of column frequency.

63: Which keyword is used with PROC MEANS to compute standard deviation?
Answer:
STDDEV/STD can be used with PROC MEANS to compute the standard deviation.
E.g.:
proc means data= exam.set1 std;
run;

64: How will you produce a report with PROC SUMMARY?
Answer:
It is possible to produce a report along with output data set with PROC SUMMARY by using the option PRINT.
E.g.:
proc summary data= exam.set1 print;

var slno set1 set2;
run;

65: Which types of values are ideal for frequency distribution?
Answer:
Categorical values / discrete values are ideal to work with frequency distribution.

E.g.: Consider the following data set exam.set1. Months are the best categorical variables as they can be used to categorize the data quickly. So month is chosen to produce frequency tables.

proc freq data= exam.set1 ;
tables month;
run;

This page is intentionally left blank

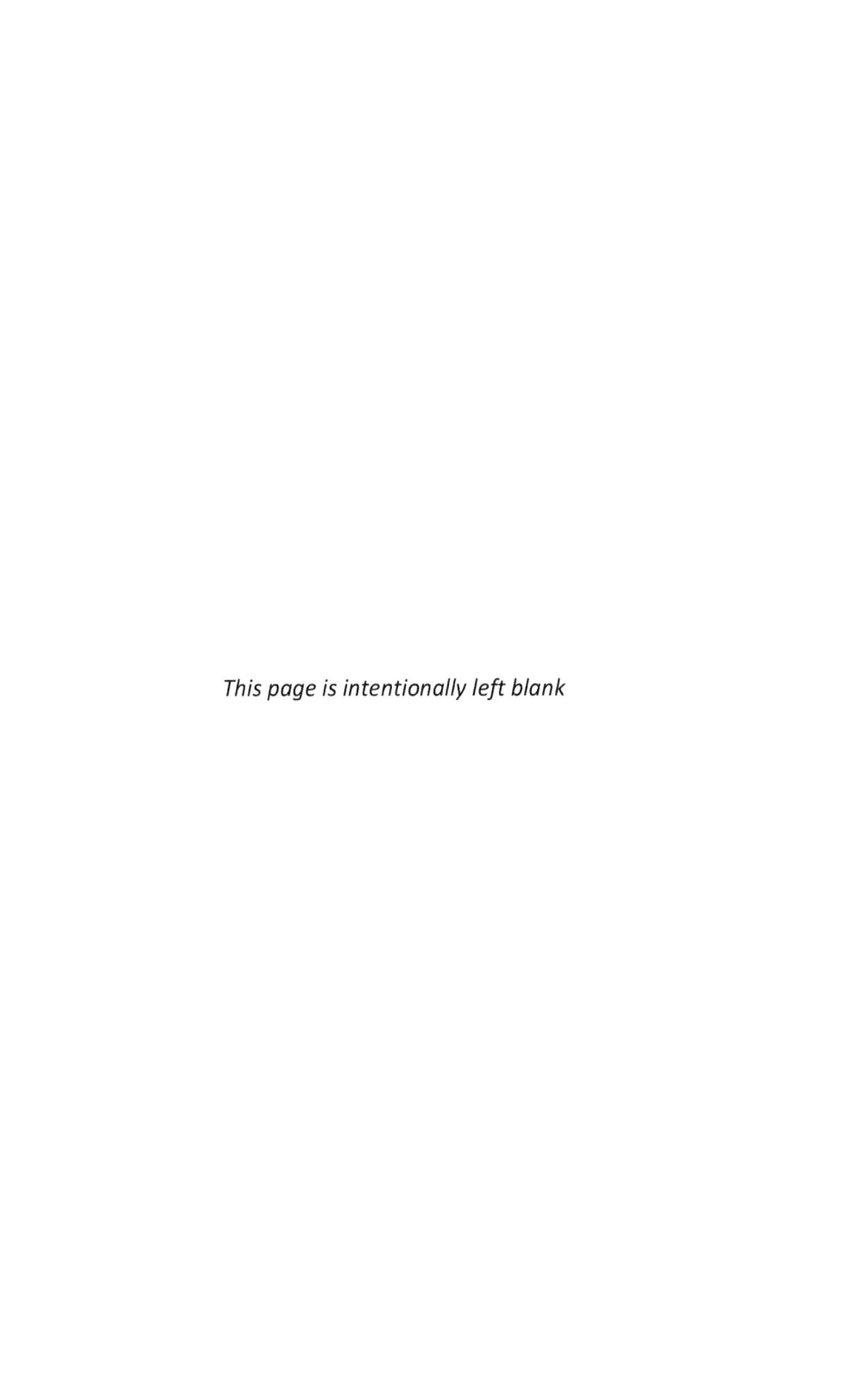

Outputs

66: Could you list some ODS destinations which are currently supported?
Answer:
HTML, LISTING, MARKUP LANGUAGES FAMILY, DOCUMENT, OUTPUT, PRINTER FAMILY & RTF are some of the ODS destinations which are currently supported by SAS.

67: How do you use the ODS statement to open LISTING destination?
Answer:
The following command can be used to open the listing destination.
ods listing;

68: Which ODS destination is open by default?
Answer:
The listing destination is open by default. Most destinations are closed by default and we need to open them at the beginning of the program.

69: Which keyword is used in ODS statements to close all the open destinations at once?
Answer:
ALL is used in the ODS close statement to close all the open destinations at once.
E.g.: The following command will close all the open destinations at once.
ods _all_ close;

70: How does ODS handle the output?
Answer:
ODS creates output objects. Output objects contain the results of steps submitted (either the data step / proc step) and information about how to display the results.

71: How do you write the ODS statements to create a simple HTML output?
Answer:
ods html body= 'D:\ sas\examset\set1.html';
ods html close;

72: Which option is used in ODS HTML statement to specify the location of storing the output?
Answer:
PATH= option can be used in ODS HTML statement to specify the location where you wish to store the HTML output.
E.g.:
ods html path = 'C:\sas';
body= 'set1.html'
contents= 'set2.html'
frame='set3.html';
proc print data= exam.questionset1;
run;
ods html close;

This page is intentionally left blank

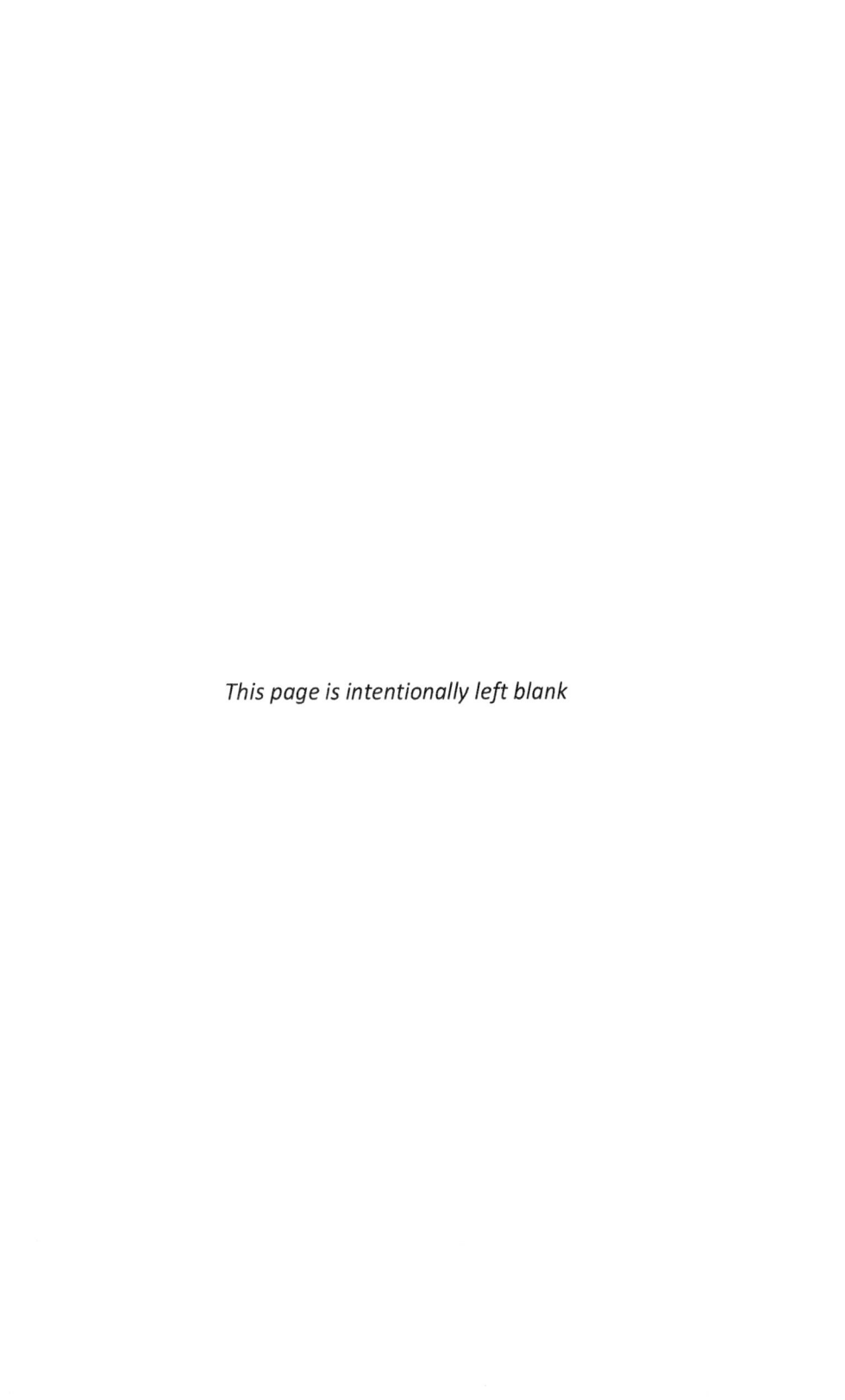

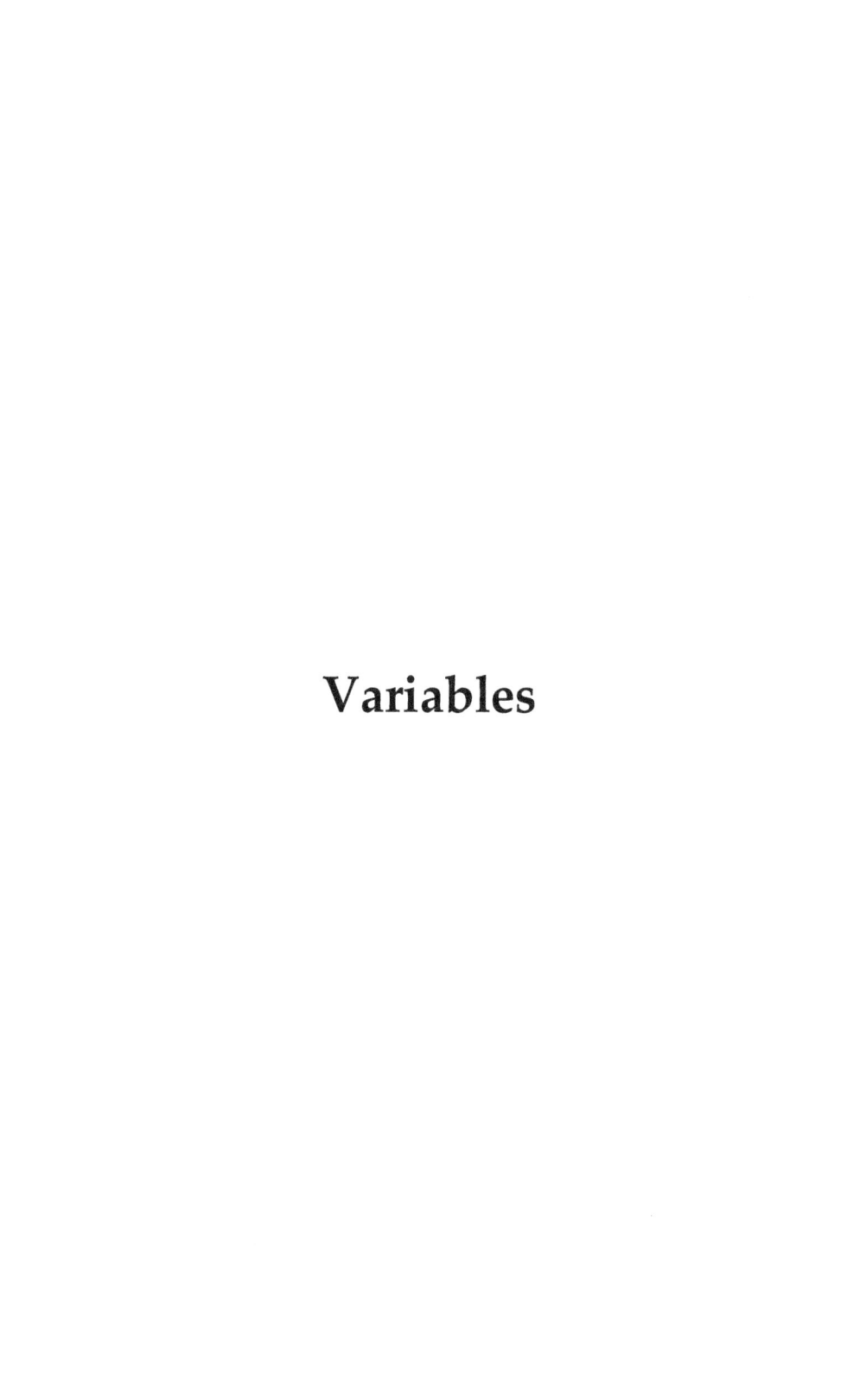

Variables

73: How does the SUM statement deal with the missing values?

Answer:

SUM statement is used to add the result of an expression to a variable. SUM statement ignores the missing values if an expression produces a missing value. If SUM statement encounters a missing value then it treats the missing value as zero and continues with the calculations.

74: How does an ASSIGNMENT statement deal with the missing values?

Answer:

While using ASSIGNMENT statement, if any missing value is encountered then the ASSIGNMENT statement assigns missing value to the variable.

75: How do you change the initial value of SUM variable?

Answer:

SUM variables are initialised to zero by default. RETAIN statement can be used to change the initial value of the sum variable.

E.g.: The following program changes the initial value of the variable setno to 543.

retain setno 543;

76: How do you consider the value of zero in SAS while using Boolean expressions?

Answer:

In SAS, the value of zero and missing values are considered to be false. Any other value is true in SAS.

77: While creating a new character variable in the ASSIGNMENT statement, how is the length of the variable determined?

Answer:
While creating a new character variable in the ASSIGNMENT statement, SAS checks the first value of the variable and allocates as many bytes of storage space as required by this first value. Thus the length of the variable will be equal to the length of first value of the variable. Remaining values of the variables are truncated or padded accordingly.

78: Is it possible to assign length to a character variable created using ASSIGNMENT statement?

Answer:
Yes, it is possible. Even though SAS allocates storage space according to the first value of the variable, it is possible to assign length using LENGTH statement.
E.g.: In the following program the variable set is assigned a length of 8 using LENGTH statement. This statement should be placed before the variable is referenced anywhere.
length set $ 8;

79: What is the function of KEEP= option?

Answer:
KEEP= option helps in keeping the variables required in a data

set. Some times during the processing of a data set, it may be required to eliminate some variables and keep some. In such cases KEEP= option helps in the purpose.

80: HOW is DROP statement used in SAS procedure?
Answer:
DROP statement cannot be used with SAS procedure steps.

81: Which form of the DO statement checks the condition before each iteration of DO loop?
Answer:
In SAS, DO WHILE statement executes statements in a loop repetitively checking the condition before each iteration of the DO loop.

82: What is the result of the following IF statement?
if setno=23 or 45;
Answer:
The above IF statement always evaluates to true. The first condition setno=23 may or may not evaluate to true but 45 is always true as it is a non-missing value and not equal to zero also.

83: Suppose you have a data set in which the variables are assigned with permanent labels. But, you are submitting a proc step in which you are assigning a new label to one of the variables. What will be displayed as the label for the variable- new one or the one which is permanently stored?

Answer:

If we are assigning temporary labels within a proc step, they override the labels which are permanently stored in the data set.

This page is intentionally left blank

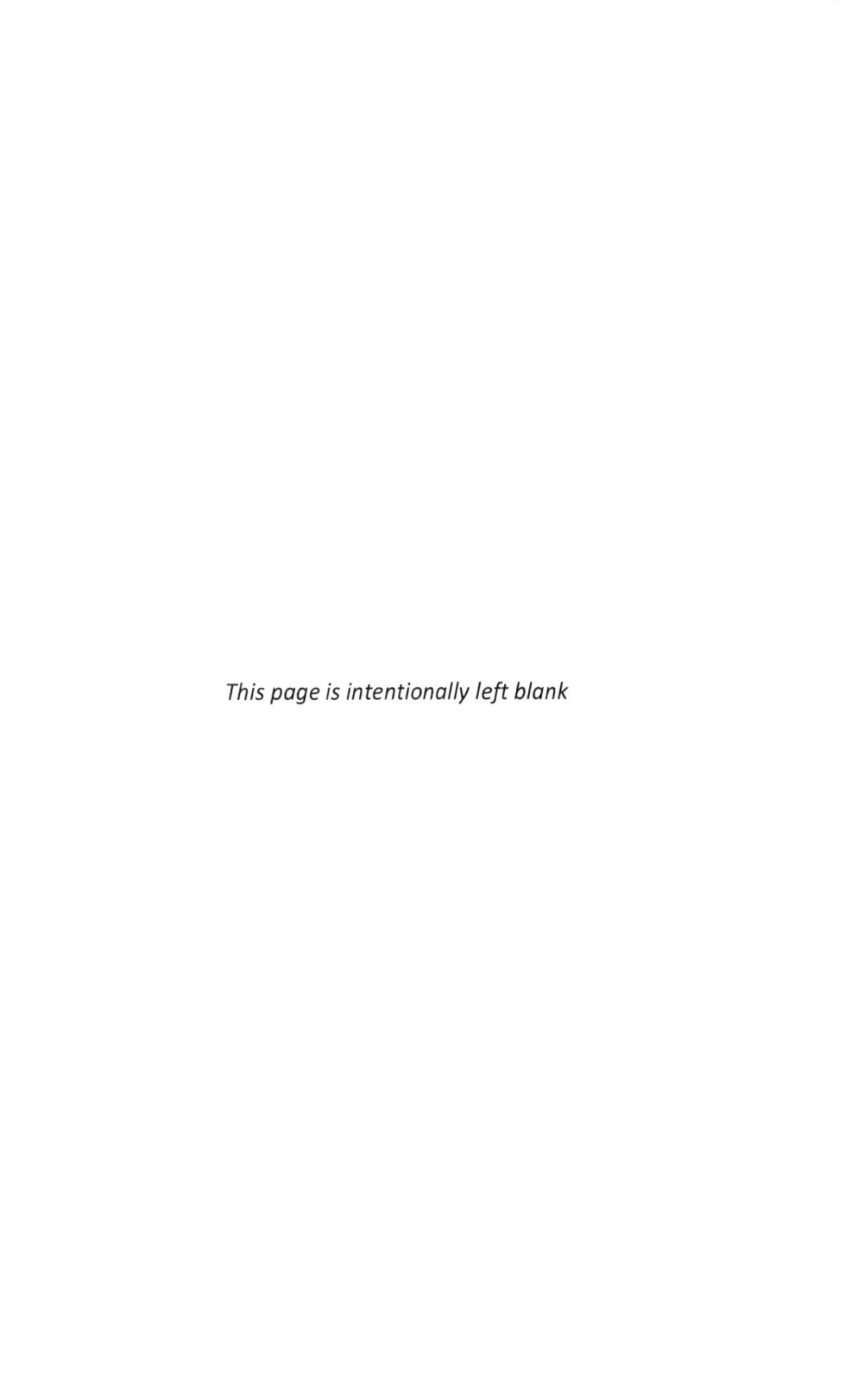

Combining Data Sets

84: How do you read a data set questionset1 which is stored in the library 'exam'?

Answer:

The following statement can be used to read the data set questionset1 stored in the library 'exam':

set exam.questionset1;

85: You might be aware of the DROP= option. What criteria should you use to decide whether to place the option in the SET statement or DATA statement?

Answer:

DROP= option is usually used when you don't want certain variables to appear in the new data set. We usually specify the DROP= option in the DATA statement if you need the variables for some processing but you don't want them to appear in the new data set. But if you don't require processing of certain variables and you don't want them to appear in the new data set also, you can use the DROP= option in the SET statement.

86: Which variables are created automatically when you are using BY statement with the SET statement?

Answer:

While using BY statement with SET statement, the data step automatically creates two variables- first.variable and last.variable for each variable in the data set. These are temporary variables.

E.g.: The following program uses SET statement with BY statement. The data step creates two temporary variables first.result and last.result

data exam.questionset1;

set exam.set2;

by result;

run;

87: How do you go straight to an observation in a data set without considering preceding observations?

Answer:

It is possible to fetch an observation directly by using POINT= option.

Suppose you want to read 5th observation from exam.questionset2 then we write the following program:

data exam.questionset4;

obs=5;

set exam.questionset3 point=obs;

output;

stop;

run;

88: What happens if we specify invalid values for POINT= variables?

Answer:

When SAS detects invalid values for the POINT= variable, it sets the automatic variable _ERROR_ to 1.

89: How do you detect an end of data set while reading data?

Answer:

To detect the end of a data set, a temporary numeric variable can be created with END= option in the SET statement. The variable is having a value of zero but the value changes to one when the SET statement reads the last observation from the data set. It is a temporary variable and is not added to the data set.

90: Which conditions have to be checked while using POINT= option?

Answer:

While using POINT= option, a STOP statement has to be used to prevent continuous looping. Since the observation is read directly and there is no end of the file condition reached, an output statement also needs to be used.

E.g.: Suppose you want to read 5th observation from exam.questionset2 then we write the following program.

data exam.questionset4;

obs=5;

set exam.questionset3 point=obs;

output;

stop;

run;

91: While performing one-to-one reading does the resulting data set contain all the observations and variables from the input data sets?

Answer:

While performing one-to-one reading, the resulting data set has all the variables from the input data sets. If the input data sets have variables with the same name then the data from the data set which was read last overrides the data which was read earlier. The number of observations will be the same as the number of observations in the smallest data set.

92: What is the maximum number of data sets which can be given as an input for APPEND procedure?
Answer:
While using APPEND procedure, only two data sets can be combined at a time.

93: How does concatenating combine the input data sets?
Answer:
When a program is submitted to concatenate two or more data sets, SAS first reads all the observations from the first data set. Then it proceeds to next data set, reads all the observations and variables and so on. Thus the new data set which is produced after concatenation will have all the observations and variables from the combining data sets.
E.g.: The following data set exam.questionset4 contains all the observations and variables from both set2 and set3.
data exam.questionset4;
    set exam.set2 exam.set3;
run;

94: What is the prerequisite for two data sets to be merged by MERGE statement?

Answer:

The two data sets must be either indexed or sorted according to the variables mentioned as BY variables. Also each BY variable must be having the same data type in all the input data sets.

95: How do you use the RENAME data set option?

Answer:

RENAME= data option is used with SET or MERGE statement. It can also be used in the data statement.

The syntax is as follows:

(RENAME=(current variable name= new variable name))

96: How many variables can be renamed at one time using RENAME= option?

Answer:

Any number of variables can be renamed at one stretch using RENAME= option.

97: How does one-to-one merging produce output?

Answer:

As the name implies one-to-one merging is identical to one-to-one reading but there are some differences. The output data set produced by one-to-one merging contains all the observations and variables from the input data sets. Also one-to-one merging uses MERGE statement rather than multiple SET statements.

98: What is the functionality of IN= data set option?

Answer:

IN= data set option is used in match-merging process to avoid those observations which do not match. This creates a temporary variable and based on the value of the variable, those observations which do not match in the two data sets (unmatching observations) are excluded.

99: What is the difference between PROC APPEND and concatenate?

Answer:

The results produced by both PROC APPEND and concatenate look identical. But concatenate produces a new data set with all the observations and variables from the input data sets. PROC APPEND simply adds the observations and variables from one data set to the base data set. PROC APPEND does not read the base data set and it does not produce a new data set as well.
E.g.: The following program concatenates two data sets and produces a new data set exam.questionset4 which contains all the observations and variables from the input data sets.
data exam.questionset4;
    set exam.set2 exam.set3;
run;
The following program appends the observations in set3 to the end of observations in set2. No new data set is produced.
proc append base=exam.set2;
    data= exam.set3;
run;

100: In which scenarios do you prefer to use the data set option KEEP= rather than using the data set option DROP=?
Answer:
The data set options KEEP= and DROP= are used for specifying the variable to be included or dropped. KEEP= option is generally used when more number of variables are to be dropped. In such cases, the number of variables to be maintained will be less; so it will be easy to list those variables with KEEP= option.

SAS Functions

101: Which function is used to convert character data values to numeric data values?

Answer:

INPUT function converts character data values to numeric data values. Syntax of the function is input(source, informat). source is the character variable or constant which needs to be converted to numeric data values. informat should be numeric so as to read the form of the values.

E.g.: The following program converts the character variable 'set' to numeric values. set is the source and it has a length of 3. So a numeric informat of 3. is used to read the values of the variable 'set'. When the data step is executed, a new numeric variable type is created.

data exam.questionset4;
    set exam.set3;
type= input(set, 3.);
run;

102: How does SAS store a date value?

Answer:

SAS stores date value as number of days from January 1, 1960 to the given date.

E.g.: Jan 1, 1961 is counted as 366 days by SAS.

103: Explain the significance of the function MDY.

Answer:

MDY is a function which is used to create a date. It takes month, day and year as input and returns a date value.

E.g.: The following program uses MDY function to create a date from the input values. The function calculates the date value, March 27, 2012 and assigns it to date variable.

data exam.questionset4;
    set exam.set3;
date= mdy(3, 27, 2012);
run;

104: What is the significance of DATE function?
Answer:
DATE function returns the current date as a SAS date value. The date function requires no arguments.

E.g.: When the following data step is submitted, a new variable 'mydate' is created. 'mydate' contains the value of current date.

data exam.questionset4;
    set exam.set3;
mydate= date();
run;

105: Which function can be used interchangeably with DATE function?
Answer:
TODAY function can be used interchangeably with DATE function. TODAY also returns the current date as a SAS date value. TODAY function requires no arguments.

E.g.: When the following data step is submitted, a new variable 'mydate' is created. 'mydate' contains the value of current date.

data exam.questionset4;

```
    set exam.set3;
mydate= today();
run;
```

106: Name some functions which provide results which are analogous to the results produced by any SAS procedure like PROC MEANS.

Answer:

SUM, MEAN, MIN, MAX, VAR are some of the functions which produce the same result which is produced by PROC MEANS.

The following example illustrates the use of one of the above function - SUM. When the following data step is submitted, a new variable 'value' is created. 'value' contains the sum of three variables.

```
data exam.questionset4;
    set exam.set3;
value= sum(x1, x2,x3);
run;
```

107: What is a target variable?

Answer:

Target variable is a variable to which the result of the function is assigned.

E.g.: In the following program the result of the DATE function is assigned to a variable 'mydate'. Hence 'mydate' is the target variable.

```
data exam.questionset4;
```

set exam.set3;
mydate= date();
run;

108: What happens when a character value is used in arithmetic operations?
Answer:
When a character value is used in arithmetic operations, SAS does an automatic conversion of the character value to numeric value. After the completion of automatic conversion, a message is written to the log indicating that automatic conversion has occurred.

E.g.: In the following program, 'set' is a character variable. But when it is used in arithmetic operation (multiplication), SAS does an automatic conversion of character values into numeric values.

data exam.questionset4;
    set exam.set3;
type= set*3;
run;

109: Is the automatic conversion of character value to numeric and vice versa permissible in WHERE statements?
Answer:
WHERE statement does not support automatic conversion. Whenever there occurs a mismatch in the WHERE comparisons, automatic conversion is not performed. SAS stops the processing and error statements are written to SAS

log.

Here in the below example a character value of '453' is assigned to the variable 'type'. But in the WHERE statement a numeric value is compared which is a wrong data type. Here an automatic conversion does not occur; instead SAS stops processing the program and error message is written to the log.

data exam.questionset4;
    set exam.set3;
type= '453';
run;
proc print data=exam.questionset4;
where type=453;
run;

110: Which function is used to extract the quarter of the year in which a given date is falling?
Answer:
The function QTR is used to extract the quarter of the year from a given date.

E.g.: In the following program QTR function is used to extract the quarter values from the variable 'start date' which holds the date values.

data exam.questionset4;
    set exam.set3;
set= qtr(startdate);
run;

111: Explain the significance of WEEKDAY function.

Answer:

The function WEEKDAY is used to extract the day of the week from a given date. The WEEKDAY function returns a numeric value from 1 to 7. 1 corresponds to Sunday, 2 corresponds to Monday and so on.

E.g.: In the following program weekday function is used to extract the day of the week from the variable, start date, which holds the date values. The weekday function returns a numeric value from 1 to 7.

data exam.questionset4;
    set exam.set3;
set= weekday(startdate);
run;

112: Explain INTCK function in detail.

Answer:

The function INTCK is used to count the number of time intervals within a specified period. The interval is specified by a character variable and it can be day, weekday, month, quarter, year etc.

E.g.: In the following program INTCK function creates a new variable, year, and assigns a value of 2 as 2 years have been elapsed between 27mar2012 and 27mar2014.

data exam.questionset4;
    set exam.set3;
years=intck('year','27mar2012'd, '27mar2014'd,);
run;

113: Which function is used to extract an integer value from a given numeric value?

Answer:

INT function can be used to extract the integer portion of a numeric value. The argument of an integer function can be numeric variable, constant or expression.

E.g.: The following program creates a variable result1. The INT function extracts the integer portion of numeric variable result and assigns it to result1.

data exam.questionset4;
    set exam.set3;
result1= int(result)
run;

114: What happens when you specify an invalid date as an argument in MDY function?

Answer:

If the argument in MDY function is specified as invalid, then MDY function assigns missing value to the target variable.

E.g.: The following program uses MDY function to create a date from the input values. Here the date specified is invalid as the month is shown to be 36 so a missing value will be assigned to the date variable.

data exam.questionset4;
    set exam.set3;
date= mdy(36, 27, 2012);
run;

115: Explain INTNX function in detail.

Answer:

The INTNX function performs calculations with date values, time values and datetime values. INTNX function increments date, time or datetime values by intervals and returns the result. Intervals can be day, weekday, month, quarter, semi year and year.

E.g.: In the following program INTNX function creates a new variable year and assigns a value corresponding to January 1, 2015.

data exam.questionset4;
    set exam.set3;
year=intnx('year','03mar2012'd,3);
run;

116: What is the functionality of TRIM function?

Answer:

The TRIM function helps in removing the trailing blanks from character values. It generally takes character variables as input argument. It is also possible to nest other functions within TRIM function. The following program illustrates the use of TRIM function. TRIM function removes the trailing blanks from the values of the variable 'quest' and assigns it to the new variable 'newquest'.

data exam.questionset4;
    set exam.set3;
newquest=trim(quest);
run;

117: Which function converts all the letters of a character expression to uppercase?

Answer:

UPCASE function is used for converting all the letters of character to uppercase. The following program illustrates the use of UPCASE function. UPCASE function converts all the characters in the variable 'question' to uppercase and assigns it to 'newquestion'.

data exam.questionset4;
    set exam.set3;
newquestion=upcase(question);
run;

118: Is TRANWRD a character function? Explain the functionality.

Answer:

TRANWRD function is a character function. It enables us to replace a pattern of characters within a string with any desired pattern of characters. In the following example, TRANWRD function is used to update the variable name. It has three arguments - 'name', the source in which function needs to operate, 'cat', the target which needs to be searched in source and 'pet', the pattern which needs to replace cat. When the below data step is submitted all the occurrences of 'cat' gets replaced by 'pet' in the variable 'name'.

data exam.questionset4;
    set exam.set3;
name= tranwrd(name, 'cat','pet');

run;

119: Which function enables you to search any string within a character variable?

Answer:

INDEX function enables to search any string within a character variable. If the string is found then it returns the position of first character of the string. If it is not found, it returns zero. The following example illustrates the use of INDEX function. 'name' is the variable in which the INDEX function looks for the occurrence of the string 'cat'. If it finds the string 'cat' then it returns the position of first character of 'cat'. If no match is found, it returns zero. Consider a situation where in one of the values of the variable name is concat. In such scenario the INDEX function returns the letter 4 as it is the starting position of first character of 'cat'.

data exam.questionset4;
    set exam.set3;
name1= index (name, 'cat',);
run;

120: Name one function which is used to concatenate the strings in SAS.

Answer:

CATX function enables us to concatenate the strings in SAS. CATX function also removes the leading or trailing blanks and inserts separators in the new value. The input parameters specified in CATX function are the strings and separator which we wish to put in the new value.

The following example illustrates the use of CATX function. CATX function concatenates two strings 'lastname' and 'firstname' and assigns it to the variable 'newname'. The separator used is ',' which indicates that in the new variable 'newname', the values of 'lastname' and 'firstname' are separated by comma.

```
data exam.questionset4;
    set exam.set3;
newname= catx(',',lastname, firstname,);
run;
```

121: What is the functionality of SCAN function?
Answer:

Suppose you have a character value, marked by delimiters and you wish to split the value into separate words. SCAN function is used primarily to achieve this and return a specified word. The following example illustrates the use of SCAN function. SCAN function is used to extract the value of last name from the variable 'name'. The values in the variable name are comma separated. So comma is specified as an input argument in the SCAN function. 1 is specified to indicate that the first word of the variable name should be extracted.

```
data exam.questionset4;
    set exam.set3;
lastname= scan(name, 1,',');
run;
```

122: Explain the significance of PROPCASE function.

Answer:

PROPCASE function is used to convert all the words in the argument to proper case. Proper case means that first letter of each word is capitalized.

The following example illustrates the use of PROPCASE function. PROPCASE function takes the variable 'result' as input argument and converts it to proper case and assigns it to the variable 'newresult'. The first letter of each word in the values of 'newresult' is capitalized.

data exam.questionset4;
    set exam.set3;
newresult= propcase(result);
run;

123: What is the output of DAY function in SAS?

Answer:

DAY function returns the day of the month (1-31) for a given date i.e. when a date value is given as an argument to the DAY function, it checks the corresponding day. If the date is 4th April 2012, it returns the value 4.

E.g.: In the following program DAY function is used to extract the day values from the variable 'startdate' which holds the date values.

data exam.questionset4;
    set exam.set3;
set= day(startdate);
run;

124: What is the default length which SCAN function assigns to the target variable?

Answer:

SCAN function assigns a length of 200 to each target variable.

125: Explain functionality of SUBSTR function.

Answer:

SUBSTR function is used to extract any number of characters from a string, starting from a specified position in the string. The following example illustrates the use of SUBSTR function. SUBSTR function is used to extract the value of a character string. As the position (second argument) is 1, the extraction starts from the first position. The third argument, number of characters to be extracted is defined as 3 which indicates that 3 letter word is to be extracted. So here SUBSTR function extracts first 3 letters from the variable month and assigns it to the variable 'newmonth'.

```
data exam.questionset4;
    set exam.set3;
newmonth= substr(month,1,3);
run;
```

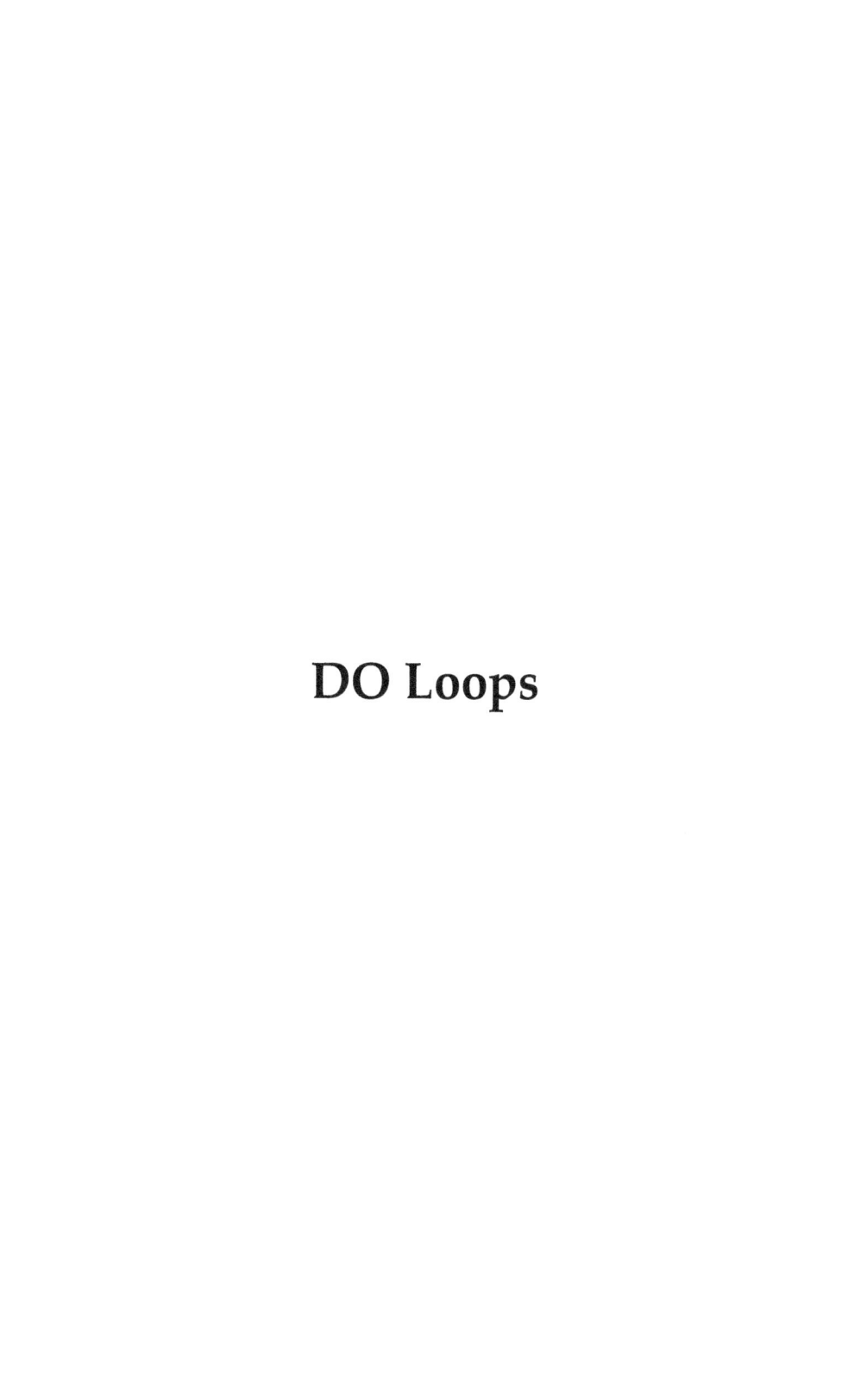

DO Loops

126: How do you construct a basic DO loop in SAS or explain the syntax of DO loop.

Answer:

DO loop helps in reducing the number of statements while performing repeated calculations. The syntax of DO loop is as follows:

do index variable=start to stop by increment;

SAS statements;

end;

where start, stop and increment can be numbers, variables or SAS expressions.

The following example shows the calculation of 'sum' variable using DO loop. 'count' is the index variable which gets incremented from 1 to 12. 'sum' statement executes 12 times within the DO loop for each iteration of the data step.

data exam.questionset4;

    sum=0;

do count=1 to 12 by 1;

sum+1;

end;

run;

127: What is the default increment value in DO loop?

Answer:

If we do not specify a BY clause in DO loop, default increment value is 1.

The following example shows the calculation of sum variable

using DO loop. 'count' is the index variable which gets incremented from 1 to 12 . 'sum' statement executes 12 times within the DO loop for each iteration of the data step. There is no BY clause specified but the count variable gets incremented by 1.

data exam.questionset4;
    sum=0;
do count=1 to 12 ;
sum+1;
end;
run;

128: Can DO loops be used to combine DATA and PROC steps?
Answer:
DO loops are data step statements and cannot be used along with PROC steps.

129: In SAS is it allowed to decrement DO loop?
Answer:
It is possible to decrement DO loop's index variable by specifying a negative value for the BY clause.
The following example shows the use of negative BY clause. The index variable gets decremented from 10 to 1. 'sum' statement gets executed 10 times within DO loop for each iteration of the data step.

data exam.questionset4;
    sum=0;

```
do count=10 to 1 by -1 ;
sum+1;
end;
run;
```

130: While specifying the number of iterations in DO loop in SAS, is it possible to list the items in series?

Answer:

It is possible to list the items in series to specify the number of iterations of DO loop. Commas can be used to separate the items in series. When the DO loop is executing, it executes for each item in the series. The items should be all character or all numeric or all variable names.

In the following example, items are listed in a series. When DO loop executes, it executes for each item in the series. Here all the items are numeric and the below loop executes for 5 times.

```
data exam.questionset4;
    sum=0;
do count=3, 7, 9, 13, 20;
sum+1;
end;
run;
```

131: Which condition has to be taken care of while specifying variable names to specify the number of iterations in DO loop?

Answer:

While specifying variable names to specify the number of

iterations in DO loop, it should be noted that the variable names should be either all character or all numeric. SAS allows only one type of variable names in a single loop. Also the variable names should not be enclosed in quotation marks.

In the following example, items are listed in a series. When DO loop executes, it executes for each item in the series. Here all the items (set1, set2, set3) are numeric and the below loop executes for 3 times.

data exam.questionset4;
    sum=0;
do count=set1, set2, set3;
sum+1;
end;
run;

132: How does a DO UNTIL loop execute in SAS?
Answer:

DO UNTIL loop executes a DO loop until an expression is found to be true. The expression is evaluated at the end of the loop. So DO UNTIL loop is executed atleast once. It executes until the expression evaluates to true.

The following example illustrates the usage of DO UNTIL loop. The following loop executes 11 times until the value of sum becomes 11, after which it stops.

data exam.questionset4;
    sum=0;
do until (sum>10);
sum+1;

end;

run;

133: Explain the DO WHILE statement.

Answer:

DO WHILE loop statement also executes DO loop based on a condition. Here the condition is evaluated at the beginning of the loop. So the loop executes only if the condition is true. If the condition specified in the DO WHILE statement is found to be false, the loop never executes.

The following example illustrates the usage of DO WHILE loop. Since this is a DO WHILE loop, condition is evaluated at the beginning of the loop. The condition is false, since the value of sum is 0. So the below loop never executes.

data exam.questionset4;

    sum=0;

do while (sum>10);

sum+1;

end;

run;

134: How do you create observation for each iteration of a DO loop?

Answer:

It is possible to create observation for each iteration of a DO loop by placing output statements inside the DO loop.

In the following example, placing an explicit output statement causes observation for each iteration of DO loop to be written to the data set. In the absence of this output statement, only the final observation would be written to the data set.

```
data exam.questionset4;
    sum=0;
do until (sum>10);
sum+1;
output;
end;
run;
```

135: Is it possible to nest DO loops in SAS?
Answer:
It is possible to nest the DO loops in SAS. Putting one DO loop inside other loop is called nesting of DO loops. It should be taken care that the index variable should be different in each DO loop and each DO loop should be ended properly with an end statement.

In the following example, the variables sum and result are initialized to zero. The first loop executes five times incrementing the value of sum. For each iteration of the outer loop, the inner DO loop executes 10 times.

```
data exam.questionset4;
    sum=0;
result=0;
do count=1 to 5 ;
sum+1;
do index=1 to 10;
result+1;
```

end;
end;
run;

Arrays

136: What is the scope of an array in SAS?

Answer:

An array is the temporary grouping of variables under the same name. The scope of an array is for the duration of data step, that is the array exists only for the duration of data step. They do not become a part of output data set.

137: What will happen if you name an array with a function name?

Answer:

If an array is given the same name as a function name, the array will function correctly but it won't be possible to use the function in the same data step in which array is defined. A warning message will appear in the log.

138: In SAS, is it possible to use array names in DROP, KEEP, LENGTH and FORMAT statements?

Answer:

No, SAS does not allow you to specify array names in DROP, KEEP, LENGTH and FORMAT statements.

139: How do you define a one dimensional array?

Answer:

An array can be defined by using an ARRAY statement. An ARRAY statement contains the name of the array, dimension of the array and the elements to be included in the array. The dimension indicates the number of elements in the array and their arrangements.

In the following example, an array result is created which has a dimension of 5. It has five numeric elements set1, set2, set3, set4 and set5.

data exam.questionset4;
set exam.questionset3;
array result {5} set1 set2 set3 set4 set5;
run;

140: How do you indicate the dimension of a one dimensional array?

Answer:

The dimension of a one dimensional array can be specified as a number in the ARRAY statement. It is also possible to specify the dimension by including an asterisk{*} in the ARRAY statement. While using asterisk you need to specify the elements to be included so that SAS determines the number of elements by counting them.

In the following example, an array result is created which has a dimension of 5. It has five numeric elements set1, set2, set3, set4 and set5.

data exam.questionset4;
set exam.questionset3;
array result {5} set1 set2 set3 set4 set5;
/* array result {*} set1 set2 set3 set4 set5;*/
run;

141: Which term do you use to specify that the array includes all the numeric variables which are defined in the current

data step?

Answer:

NUMERIC should be used in the ARRAY statement to specify that all the numeric variables are to be included in the array.

In the following example, an array result is created with all numeric variables used in the data step.

data exam.questionset4;

set exam.questionset3;

array result {*} _numeric_;

run;

142: Which function is used to determine number of elements in an array?

Answer:

DIM function returns the number of elements in an array. It takes input parameter as an array name. It can be used as a counter in the DO loop as well.

In the following example, an array result is created with an ARRAY statement. DIM function is used to determine the stop value in the DO loop. The DIM function returns a value of 5 as there are five elements in the array result.

data exam.questionset4;

set exam.questionset3;

array result {*} set1 set2 set3 set4 set5;

do count=1 to dim(result);

result{i}= result{i}*2;

end;

run;

143: How do you define an array of character variables in SAS?
Answer:
An array of character variables can be defined by adding a $ sign in the array statement.

In the following example, a character array result is created with an ARRAY statement. The array has five elements.

data exam.questionset4;
set exam.questionset3;
array result {5} $ set1 set2 set3 set4 set5;
do count=1 to dim(result);
result{i}= result{i}*2;
end;
run;

144: How do you assign initial values to the array element?
Answer:
It is possible to assign initial values to the array elements using the ARRAY statement.

In the following example, an array result is created with an ARRAY statement. The array has five elements. The initial values of each of the five elements are set to 100, 200, 300, 400 and 500.

data exam.questionset4;
set exam.questionset3;
array result {5} set1 set2 set3 set4 set5 (100 200 300 400 500);

do count=1 to dim(result);
result{i}= result{i}*2;
end;
run;

145: How do you define a two-dimensional array?

Answer:

It is possible to define a two dimensional array by specifying the number of elements in both the dimension in the ARRAY statement. The first dimension specifies the number of rows and second dimension specifies the number of columns.

In the following example, a two-dimensional array result is created with an ARRAY statement. The array has six elements. The array elements are grouped into 2 rows and 3 columns. They are grouped according to the order in which they are listed. set1, set2, set3 forms first row and remaining i.e. set4, set5 and set6 forms second row.

data exam.questionset4;
set exam.questionset3;
array result {2,3}   set1 set2 set3 set4 set5 set6;
run;

Raw Data

146: Define nonstandard numeric data.

Answer:

Nonstandard numeric data can be defined as the data which contains:
- a) special characters such as percentage signs, dollar signs and commas
- b) date value or time value
- c) data in fraction, binary and hexadecimal form

147: What is free format data?

Answer:

Free format data is that data which is not arranged in columns. The values of a particular field do not begin and end in the same column.

The following shows an example of a part of free format data. Note that the values of the fields do not end and begin in the same column.

author1	author2	value
charles	james	255000
Dickenson	Thomas	55555
Cameroon	Bill	5000

148: Which features of column input allow it to be used for reading raw data?

Answer:

Column input has several features which enables it to be used for reading raw data. They are as follows:
- a) It can be used to read the character values which

contain embedded blanks.
b) A blank field is considered as a missing value. It does not cause other fields to be read incorrectly.
c) Fields need not be always separated by blanks or other delimiters.
d) Fields can be re-read. Also parts of fields can be re-read.

149: Which are the two input styles which SAS uses for reading data in fixed fields?

Answer:

SAS uses two input styles - column input and formatted input for reading data in fixed fields. Column input is used to read standard data in fixed fields while formatted input can be used to read both standard and non standard data.

The following example illustrates the use of column input. The input statement reads the value of the variable 'slno' which is spread from column 1 to column 4. Next it moves the pointer to column 5 and the values of the column author is read which in turn occupies columns 5 to column 12.

Column input

data exam.questionset3;

infile questfile;

input slno 1-4 author $ 5-12;

run;

The following example illustrates the use of formatted input while reading the raw data with @ pointer control. The input statement reads the value of the variable 'slno' at column 1.

Next @ pointer control moves the pointer to column 5 and the values of the column author is read.

Formatted input

data exam.questionset3;

infile questfile;

input @1 slno 4. @5 author $ 7.;

run;

150: Which parameters are to be mentioned in the input statement while using formatted input?

Answer:

Formatted input enables us to read both standard and nonstandard data in fixed fields. The following parameters are to be included while using formatted input:

a) Column pointer control: They are of two types - @n which moves the pointer to a specific column number indicated by the value of n and +n which moves the input pointer relative to the current column.

b) Variable name: Variable name which is to be created in the data set after reading the raw file.

c) Informat: This specifies how the data is read.

The following example illustrates the use of formatted input while reading the raw data with two pointer controls. The first program uses @ pointer control while second program uses + pointer control. The input statement reads the value of the variable 'slno' at column 1. Next @ pointer control moves the pointer to column 5 and the values of the column author is read.

Formatted input using @ pointer control

data exam.questionset3;

infile questfile;

input @1 slno 4. @5 author $ 7.;

run;

The following example illustrates the use of formatted input while reading the raw data using + pointer control. The input statement reads the value of the variable 'slno' at column 1. After the values of 'slno' are read the column pointer is moved 1 column ahead (+1) to read the values of author.

Formatted input using + pointer control

data exam.questionset3;

infile questfile;

input @1 slno 4. +1 author $ 7.;

run;

151: Which numeric informat can be used if the data contains commas, percentage signs, dashes and dollars?

Answer:

COMMAw.d informat can be used to read the numeric values and it also removes embedded blanks, commas, dashes and dollar sign. The COMMAw.d informat has 3 parts:

a) Name of the informat which is comma

b) Value which is used to specify the width of the field followed by the period

c) Value which is used to indicate the number of decimal places

E.g.: COMMA9.2 informat can be used to read the nonstandard

numeric data with width of 9 and containing 2 decimal places.

152: What is fixed length record format?
Answer:
An external file can have different types of record format. Record format specifies how records are arranged in an external file. Fixed length records are one type of record format. External files with fixed length record format have an end of record marker after certain fixed number of columns. Normal record length in external files is usually 80 columns.

153: Describe the significance of PAD option.
Answer:
PAD option is usually used to avoid the problems while reading variable length records using column/formatted input. The PAD option can be specified in the infile statement and it pads each of the records with blanks so that all the records in the external file have same length.

The following example illustrates the use of formatted input reading an external file specified by the fileref 'questfile' with PAD option. Since the file has variable record length, PAD option pads each of the records with blanks so that all are of same length. This is particularly useful when there are missing values at the end of each record.

Formatted input using @ pointer control
data exam.questionset3;
infile questfile;
input @1 slno 4. @5 author $ 7.;

run;

154: Which parameters are to be mentioned in the input statement while using LIST input?

Answer:

LIST input is used for reading standard as well as nonstandard free format data. The following parameters are to be used in the input statement while reading the data with LIST input:

a) Variable name: specifies the variable name whose value is to be read
b) $: This specifies that the variable is character. This is used only while reading character variables.

The following example illustrates the use of LIST input while reading raw data.

LIST input
data exam.questionset3;
infile questfile;
input slno author $;
run;

155: Explain the significance of DLM= option.

Answer:

DLM= option is used in the infile statement to specify any other delimiter other than blank. Blank is the default delimiter. So it is always advisable to specify the usage of any other delimiter. The following example illustrates the use of DLM= option. Comma is specified as a delimiter. Any number of characters upto 200 can be used to specify delimiters.

```
data exam.questionset3;
infile questfile dlm=',';
input slno author $ ;
run;
```

156: Is it possible to specify a range of character variables in the input statement, if the values are sequential?

Answer:

Yes, it is possible to specify a range of character variables in the input statement if the values of the variables are sequential. While using list input to read these values, both the range of character variables and dollar sign must be enclosed in parenthesis.

In the following example, the input statement creates 5 character variables - author1, author2, author3, author4 and author5.

```
data exam.questionset3;
infile questfile dlm=',';
input (author1-author5) ($) ;
run;
```

157: What are the main limitations of LIST input?

Answer:

LIST input when used in default form has many limitations:
   a) Data should be standard numeric/character.
   b) Character values must not contain embedded delimiters.
   c) Character values which are longer than 8 characters will

get truncated.

d) Missing values must be represented by some character like period.

158: Which option enables you to read the missing values at the end of the record?
Answer:
MISSOVER option can be used in the infile statement to read the missing values at the end of the record. Without MISSOVER option in the infile statement, the list input goes to next record if it does not find values for all the variables in the current line. MISSOVER option prevents SAS from going to next record in such cases and values which are not found are set to missing.

The following example illustrates the use of MISSOVER option. MISSOVER option prevents SAS from going to next record if it does not find values for all the variables in the current record. Values which are not found are set to missing. Thus MISSOVER option enables to read the missing values at the end of the record.

data exam.questionset3;
infile questfile missover;
input slno author $;
run;

159: Which option is specified to read the missing values at the beginning or middle of the record?
Answer:

DSD option can be used in the infile statement to read the missing values at the middle of the record. DSD option also enables you to read the missing values at the beginning of the record provided a delimiter precedes a first value in the record. The following example illustrates the use of DSD option. DSD enables to read the missing values at the beginning or the middle of the record.

data exam.questionset3;
infile questfile dsd;
input slno author $;
run;

160: How does the DSD option affect the way SAS treats delimiters when used with list input?

Answer:

DSD option affects the way SAS treats delimiters when used with list input in the following ways:

DSD option sets the default delimiter to comma.

It treats two consecutive delimiters as a missing value and thus helps in identifying the missing values in between the record.

It helps in removing the quotation marks from the values.

161: What happens when list input is used to read character variables whose value has length more than 8?

Answer:

When list input is used to read the values of character variables whose value has length more than 8, the values of the variables get truncated to 8 when they are written to program data vector and after that to data set.

The above limitation can be overcome by writing a length statement preceding the input statement.

E.g.: In the following program the LENGTH statement which precedes the input statement defines the length and type for the character variable - author. A length of 20 has been assigned to the variable 'author'. Since LENGTH statement has been added in the following program, even those values of the 'author' which are longer than 8 characters are correctly read into the data set. In the absence of LENGTH statement those values of 'author' which are greater than 8 characters will get truncated to 8.

data exam.questionset3;

infile questfile dsd;

length author $ 20;

input slno author $;

run;

162: Which modifier is used with LIST input to read the character values having embedded blanks?

Answer:

LIST input can be made more versatile by modifying it. An ampersand (&) modifier can be used with LIST input to read the values of character variables with embedded blanks.

E.g.: In the following program the LENGTH statement which precedes the input statement defines the length and type for the character variable - author. The variable 'author' may contain values with embedded blanks like Charles Dickens.

Use of '&' modifier enables us to read the value of 'author' which contains embedded blanks.

data exam.questionset3;

infile questfile dsd;

length author $ 20;

input slno author & ;

run;

163: Which modifier is used along with LIST input to read the nonstandard data values?

Answer:

LIST input can be made more versatile by modifying it. A colon (:) modifier can be used with LIST input to read the non standard data values which are not having embedded blanks. E.g.: In the following program 'value' is a field which contains non standard numeric values like comma and does not contain embedded blanks. So the colon (:) modifier when used in the input statement enables us to read the values of the variable 'value' properly using an informat comma.

data exam.questionset3;

infile questfile dsd;

length author $ 20;

input slno author & value : comma. ;

run;

164: How does an informat function when used with formatted input?

Answer:

INFORMAT works differently when used with modified list input as well as formatted input. With formatted input, informat determines the length of a variable as well as the number of columns which are being read.

E.g.: The following example illustrates the use of formatted input while reading raw data with @ pointer control. The input statement reads the value of the variable 'author'. Here an informat 7. is used to read the values of the variable 'author'. Input statement reads the same number of columns (7 columns) from each record.

Formatted input

data exam.questionset3;

infile questfile;

input @1 slno 4. @5 author $ 7.;

run;

165: How does an informat function when used with modified list input?

Answer:

Informat work differently when used with modified list input as well as formatted input. The informat in modified list input determines only the length of the variable not the number of columns which are being read.

Eg: In the following program the informat used ($12.) determines only the length of the variable 'author'. Here the raw data values are read until two consecutive blanks are encountered.

data exam.questionset3;

infile questfile dsd;
length author $ 20;
input slno author & $12. ;
run;

166: What all parameters must be mentioned while using PUT statement with LIST output?

Answer:
The PUT statement can be used along with LIST output to create free format raw data files. The following parameters are to be included:

a) Variable name: Variable specifies which variable you need to write to raw data file
b) : (colon): colon is specified before a format (it is optional and used only when format is specified)
c) format: This specifies which format to use for writing the values to the raw data file

E.g.: In the following program a raw data file 'questfile' is created using the data set exam.questionset3. The program illustrates the use of PUT statement. date9. format is used for writing the variable 'startdate'.

data _null_ ;
　　set exam.questionset3;
　　file 'c:\sas\questfile';
put slno author startdate : date9.;
run;

167: Is it allowed to mix three types of input styles to read the

raw data?

Answer:

Yes, it is allowed to mix three types of input styles - column input, formatted input and list input to read the raw data. In fact to read some types of raw data files, it is required to mix three types of input styles.

E.g.: In the following program three types of input styles are mixed to read from a raw data file. In the raw data file, the values of 'slno' are standard and data are located in fixed columns. So column input is used to read the values of the variable 'slno'. The field 'author' is also standard but this requires an informat. So formatted input is used to read the values of the variable 'author'. The third field 'startdate' does not begin or end in the same column. So list input is used to read the values of 'startdate'.

data exam.questionset3;

infile questfile dsd;

length author $ 20;

input slno 1-3 @5 author $12. startdate : date9. ;

run;

168: How do you use a PUT statement to write a character string to a raw data file?

Answer:

It is possible to write a character string to a raw data file using PUT statement by adding the string to PUT statement. The string must be enclosed in quotation marks.

E.g.: In the following program a raw data file 'questfile' is created using the data set exam.questionset3. In this program the string to be written to the raw data file is mentioned in the PUT statement.

```
data _null_ ;
    set exam.questionset3;
    file 'c:\sas\questfile';
put  'Author is ' author 'The start date is 'startdate : date9.;
run;
```

169: Is it possible to skip certain fields while using list input?
Answer:
While using list input, it is not possible to skip the fields in between. Also list does not allow re-reading of fields. Fields must be read in order from left to right while using list input. Fields must be separated by one blank or any other delimiter.

Date and Time Value

170: While storing dates, does SAS make adjustments for daylight saving time?

Answer:

No, SAS does not make adjustments for daylight saving time. SAS makes adjustments for leap years but ignores leap seconds.

171: Explain DATEw informat in detail.

Answer:

Datew. informat reads the date values in the form ddmmmyy or ddmmmyyyy where:

dd is an integer value representing day of the month. It can range from 0-31.

mmm represents first three letters of a month's name

yy or yyyy represents the year

E.g.: Date9. informat reads the data values in the form ddmmmyyyy (24Apr2012).

172: What is the minimum acceptable field width for TIMEw. informat?

Answer:

Timew. informat requires a minimum acceptable field width of 5. If you specify a width value which is less than 5, an error message is generated in the log.

E.g.: This example is to show the use of TIMEw. informat Time5. informat reads the data values in the form hh:mm(10:20) where:

hh represents hour and can range from 00 to 23

mm represents minutes and can range from 00 to 59.

173: Explain WORDDATEw. format.

Answer:

WORDDATEw. is a date format which writes the values in the form 'monthname dd, yyyy' where:

dd represents the day of the month and can range from 1 to 31

yyyy represents year

E.g.: In the following example, the values of the variable 'startdate' are stored in the form monthname dd, yyyy (April 24, 2012)

data exam.questionset3;

infile questfile dsd;

length author $ 20;

input slno 1-3 @5 author $12. startdate : date9. ;

format startdate worddate14.;

run;

174: How does YEARCUTOFF= option affect the four digit year values?

Answer:

YEARCUTOFF= system option does not affect the four digit year values. Four digit year values are read correctly. While working with two digit year data it is always necessary to check the default value of YEARCUTOFF= system option and change it if necessary.

175: Explain WEEKDATEw. format.

Answer:

WEEKDATEw. is a date format which writes the values in the format which displays the day of the week, month, day and year. The general format in which values are written is: 'Day of the week, monthname dd, yyyy' where

dd represents the day of the month and can range from 1 to 31

yyyy represents year

E.g.: In the following example, the values of the variable 'startdate' are stored in the form day of the week, monthname dd, yyyy (Tue, Apr 24, 2012)

data exam.questionset3;

infile questfile dsd;

length author $ 20;

input slno 1-3 @5 author $12. startdate : date9. ;

format startdate weekdate17.;

run;

176: Explain TIMEw. informat.

Answer:

TIMEw. is a date informat which reads the values in the form hh:mm:ss.ss where

hh is an integer which represents the hour and it ranges from 0 to 23

mm is an integer which represents minutes and it ranges from 0 to 59

ss.ss represents seconds and hundredths of seconds respectively. This value is optional.

E.g.: In the following program the informat used (Time11.)

reads the values of the variable 'starttime' in the form hh:mm:ss.ss. So a sample value would be 10:50:01.34

data exam.questionset3;
infile questfile dsd;
length author $ 20;
input slno author & $12. starttime Time11. ;
run;

177: How does SAS store date and time and what is the advantage?

Answer:

SAS stores date and time as numeric values. SAS date value is counted as number of days from Jan1, 1960 to the given date. When a SAS informat is used to read a date, SAS converts it into a numeric value. A SAS time value is counted as number of seconds since midnight. The greatest advantage of storing date and time as numeric value is that they can be used in numeric calculations just like any other numeric variable. This feature is not available in most of the programming languages.

This page is intentionally left blank

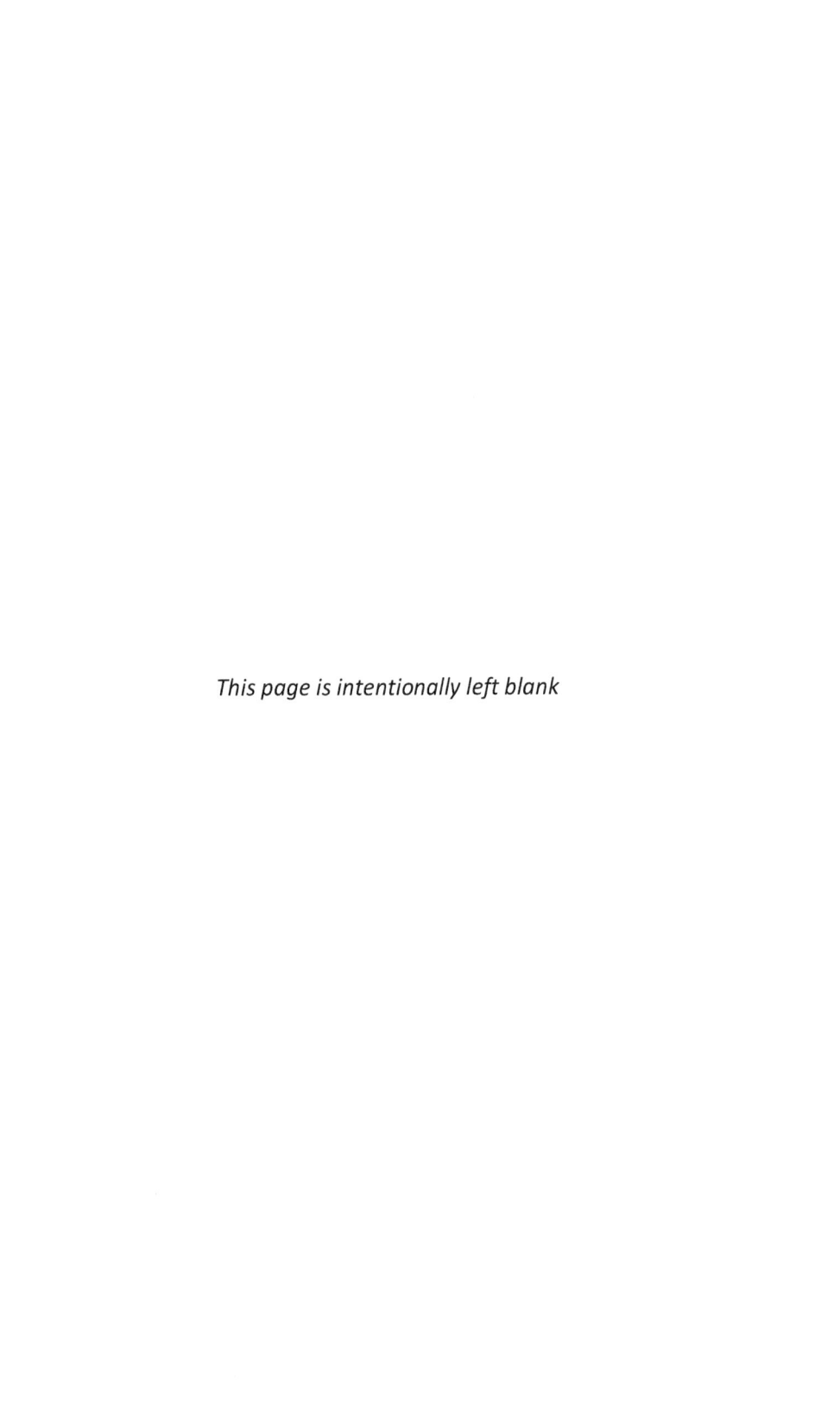

Line Pointer Controls

178: Explain #n line pointer control in SAS.

Answer:

#n specifies the number of line to which you intend to move the pointer control in SAS. Suppose the data which you wish to read has observations spread over different lines, #n pointer helps in reading the records in any order. This has to be mentioned in the input statement.

E.g.: In the following program a data set exam.questionset3 is created from the file specified by 'questfile'. In the raw data file a single observation is spread over 4 lines. So use of #n line pointer enables us to read the 'slno' first by specifying #4. 'slno' is in 4th line in the raw data file. Next we wish to go to first line to read the value of 'author1'. So #1 is specified. The value of 'author2' is in the third line in the raw data file. So we use #3 to move to 3rd line. Finally to read the value of 'author3' which is in the second line, #2 pointer is specified.

data exam.questionset3;
infile questfile;
input #4 slno
#1 author1 $
#3 author2 $
#2 author3 $;
run;

179: Explain forward slash(/) line pointer control in SAS.

Answer:

Forward slash (/) line pointer is used to specify the location of a line relative to the current line. Forward slash (/) is used to read the records sequentially. This needs to be mentioned in the input statement and it moves the pointer to the next line.

E.g.: In the following program a data set exam.questionset3 is created from the file specified by 'questfile'. In the raw data file a single observation is spread over 4 lines. Here the input statement reads the value of 'slno' from the first line. Then the forward slash operator (/) moves the line pointer to second line .Value of 'author1' is read from second record and forward slash operator moves the line pointer control to third line. Value of 'author2' is read and again the / operator moves the pointer to 4th line thereby reading the value of 'author3'.

data exam.questionset3;

infile questfile;

input slno/

author1 $/

author2 $/

author3 $;

run;

180: Is it possible to combine both the line pointer controls (#n and /) in a SAS program to read the data both sequentially and non-sequentially?

Answer:

Yes, it is possible to combine both the line pointer controls (#n and /) in a SAS program to read the data both sequentially and non-sequentially.

E.g.: In the following program a data set exam.questionset3 is created from the file specified by 'questfile'. In the raw data file a single observation is spread over 4 lines. Here the input statement reads the value of 'slno' from the fourth line with the help of #4 line pointer control. Then the #1 line pointer control moves the line pointer to first line and reads the value of 'author1'. Forward slash operator moves the line pointer control to second line. Value of 'author2' is read and again the / operator moves the pointer to third line thereby reading the value of 'author3'.

data exam.questionset3;
infile questfile;
input #4 slno
#1 author1 $/
author2 $/
author3 $;
run;

181: While reading a file which contains multiple records per observation, what all things need to be considered?
Answer:
SAS uses line pointer controls to read multiple records per observation. The following points needs to be considered while reading:
  a) The input file should contain the same number of records for each observation that is created.
  b) All the observations must be spread over equal number of lines.
  c) A semicolon must be placed after the end of complete input statement.

d) SAS statements can spread over different lines.

E.g.: In the following program a data set exam.questionset3 is created from the file specified by 'questfile'. In the raw data file a single observation is spread over 4 lines. This is applicable for all the observations in the raw data file. Also the semi-colon is placed at the end of input statement after all the observations are read.

data exam.questionset3;
infile questfile;
input #4 slno
#1 author1 $/
author2 $/
author3 $;
run;

182: Explain the significance of REMOVE statement
Answer:
REMOVE statement is used to delete an observation from a SAS data set. It is used with a MODIFY statement.

E.g.: The following program shows an example of REMOVE statement. This deletes an observation from exam.questionset1 whose value of 'slno' is equal to 2050.

data exam.questionset1;
modify exam.questionset1;
if slno=2050 then remove;
run;

183: Explain the trailing (@) line hold specifier.

Answer:

Sometimes the raw data file may contain multiple observations per record. So while using input statement, we need to hold the current record until each set of data is read and written to data set as separate observations. This is accomplished by using line hold specifiers. The Trailing (@) sign holds the record for execution of next input statement.

E.g.: In the following program a data set exam.questionset3 is created from the file specified by 'questfile'. The file structure is such that each record consists of one serial number and four authors. Here we are planning to create one observation for each author in the new data set. So, in the new data set each observation is planned to have a serial number and one author. The first input statement reads the value of 'slno' and holds the record for reading the subsequent values of authors. Since there are four values of authors a DO loop is built to read each value of author. So each observation would have 'slno' and value of 'author'.

```
data exam.questionset3;
    infile questfile;
input slno  $ @;
    do i=1 to 4;
    input author & $12. @;
    output;
    end;
run;
```

184: Explain double trailing (@@) sign in detail.

Answer:

Sometimes the raw data file may contain multiple observations per record. So while using input statement, we need to hold the current record until each set of data is read and written to data set as separate observations. This is accomplished by using line hold specifiers. The double trailing (@@) sign holds the record for execution of next input statement, even across iterations of a data step.

E.g.: In the following program a data set exam.questionset3 is created from the file specified by 'questfile'. The input file structure is such that each record consists of three sets of 'slno' and 'author'. Since each record consist of three sets of values, data step must execute 3 times for each record. The input statement reads the value of 'slno' and 'author' and holds the current record by using double trailing (@@). The values are written to the program data vector and the control again returns to the top of data step. In the next iteration of data step, next set of values (next values of 'slno' and 'author') are read from the same record.

data exam.questionset3;
    infile questfile;
input slno author & $12. @@;
run;

185: When is a record which is held by double trailing (@@) line hold specifier released?

Answer:

A record which is held by the double trailing sign (@@) is

released when one of the following occurs:
- a) The input pointer moves past the end of the record i.e. the input pointer moves to the next record.
- b) An input which has no line hold specifier executes. (eg for an input statement without any line hold specifier : input slno author & $12.;)

186: In which situations is double trailing (@@) not allowed?
Answer:
Double trailing (@@) line hold specifier should not be used with @ pointer control, column input or with MISSOVER option.

187: When is a record which is held by single trailing (@) line hold specifier released?
Answer:
A record which is held by the single trailing sign (@) is released when the control returns to the top of data step for next iteration. It does not hold the record across iterations of the data step.

188: Consider the situation where a record is held by a single trailing (@) sign and another input statement which has an (@) executes?
Answer:
Even if during the holding of a record, another input statement with a single trailing(@) executes, there is no impact and the holding effect is still on.

189: How do you deal with records with varying number of fields while using single trailing sign(@)?
Answer:
While using single trailing sign (@) line hold specifier, if records are having varying number of fields, MISSOVER option is used in the INFILE statement. Here, as the records are having varying number of fields, they are considered as records with missing values at the end of the record.

E.g.: In the following program a data set exam.questionset3 is created from the file specified by 'questfile'. The file structure is such that first record is having 3 values (slno, author, author) and second record has two values (slno, author). Here the input statement reads the value of 'slno' and first value of 'author'. The trailing sign (@) holds the record so that subsequent values of author can be read. MISSOVER option prevents reading past the end of the record.

data exam.questionset3;
infile questfile missover;
input slno author & $12. @;
run;

190: Explain STOPOVER option in detail.
Answer:
External files may contain raw data which may contain variable length record or records having missing values. While reading such data, SAS may not be able to find the values for all the variables specified in the input statement. When no option is used in the INFILE statement, SAS goes to next record

to fetch the values of current observation. This may lead to inaccurate data in the output data set. STOPOVER is one of the options which helps to control how SAS reads past the end of the line. STOPOVER option causes SAS to stop processing when it does not find the values for all the variables specified in the input statement. When sufficient values for all the variables are not there, use of this option causes the value of error variable (_ERROR_) to be set to 1.

E.g.: In the following program a data set exam.questionset3 is created from the file specified by 'questfile'. While reading the raw data file, if any record contains no values for either 'slno' or 'author' the use of STOPOVER function causes the data step to stop processing.

data exam.questionset3;
infile questfile stopover;
input slno author & $12.;
run;

191: While reading the data from an external file, which option is used to determine the end of the file condition?
Answer:
It is possible to determine if the current record is the last record in the external file by using END= option in the INFILE statement. Like other automatic variables, the value of END= variable is not written to the data set.

E.g.: In the following program a data set exam.questionset3 is created from the file specified by 'questfile'. In this example end= option creates a temporary variable last. The variable is numeric and the value changes to 1 when the end of the file is reached.

data exam.questionset3;
infile questfile end=last;
input slno author & $12.;
if last then output;
run;

192: Explain FLOWOVER option in detail.
Answer:
External files may contain raw data which may contain variable length records or records having missing values. While reading such data, SAS may not be able to find the values for all the variables specified in the input statement. FLOWOVER option is the default behaviour of input statement. When SAS is not able to find the values of all variables in the current record, it moves to the next record and attempts to find the values to assign to the rest of the variable names in the input statement.

Eg: In the following program a data set exam.questionset3 is created from the file specified by questfile. While reading the raw data file, if any record contains no values for either slno or author the use of FLOWOVER function causes the data step to move to next record and attempt to find the value for all the variables.

data exam.questionset3;
infile questfile flowover;
input slno author & $12.;

run;

193: Explain TRUNCOVER option in detail.

Answer:

TRUNCOVER is an INFILE option which enables the data step to assign a raw data value to a variable even if it is shorter than what is expected by the input statement. If the data step is unable to find the values for the variable at the end of input record, then SAS assigns missing value to that variable.

E.g.: In the following program a data set exam.questionset3 is created from the file specified by 'questfile'. In this example even though the length of the variable 'setnumber' is expected to be 12 by the input statement, the use of TRUNCOVER statement causes the values which are shorter than 12 also to be read.

data exam.questionset3;
infile questfile truncover;
input setnumber 12.;
run;

194: Explain the LINESIZE option.

Answer:

LINESIZE is an INFILE option which is used to specify the record length which is available to the input statement. The value of LINESIZE can range from 1 to 32,767. If input statement attempts to read past the value which is specified by the LINESIZE= option, then the output depends on the other options specified in the INFILE statement (FLOWOVER,

MISSOVER, STOPOVER or TRUNCOVER). FLOWOVER is the default.

E.g.: In the following program a data set exam.questionset3 is created from the file specified by 'questfile'. The linesize is limited to 72.

data exam.questionset3;
infile questfile linesize=72 flowover;
input setnumber 12.;
run;

195: Is it possible to create more than one data set in a single data step?

Answer:

Yes it is possible to create more than one data set using a single data step. This can be achieved by mentioning the names of data sets to be created in the data statement.

E.g.: In the following simple program three data sets are created: exam.questionset3 , exam.questionset4 and exam.questionset5 by reading the input data set exam.questionset2.

data exam.questionset3 exam.questionset4 exam.questionset5;
set exam.questionset2;
run;

196: How do you rename one or more data sets in the same library?

Answer:

It is possible to rename one or more data sets in the same

library using change statement in datasets procedure.

E.g.: The following example renames two datasets in the SAS data library 'exam'. The following program starts the datasets procedure and changes the name of the dataset questionset1 to set1 and the name of the dataset questionset2 to set2. As it is processed, a statement is written to the log stating that the datasets have been renamed.

proc datasets library=exam;
change questionset1=set1 questionset2=set2;
quit;

197: How do you modify a label which was permanently assigned in a data step previously?
Answer:
It is possible to modify a label which was previously assigned in a data step by using MODIFY statement and its subordinate LABEL statement in datasets procedure.

E.g.: The following program starts the dataset procedure and specifies the input library to be 'exam'. MODIFY statement specifies the name of the dataset. The variable 'author' gets new label 'technical author'.

proc datasets library=exam;
modify questionset1;
label author='technical author';
quit;

198: Is it possible to rename variables in a dataset using datasets procedure?

Answer:

It is possible to rename variables of a dataset by using MODIFY statement and its subordinate RENAME statement in datasets procedure.

E.g.: The following program starts the dataset procedure and specifies the input library to be 'exam'. MODIFY statement specifies the name of the dataset whose variable needs to be renamed. The variable 'author1' gets renamed to 'techauthor1'.

proc datasets library=exam;
modify questionset1;
rename author1=techauthor1;
quit;

199: Is it possible to copy the data sets from one library to another using programming statements?
Answer:

It is possible to copy specific data sets from one library to another by using copy statement in datasets procedure.

E.g.: The following program starts the data set procedure and specifies the input library to be 'exam'. COPY statement specifies the name of the library from which data set is to be copied in the IN= option and also specifies the name of the library to which the dataset is to be copied in OUT= option. SELECT statement specifies the name of the dataset. Here the dataset 'questionset1' is to be copied from 'exam' library to 'finalexam' library.

proc datasets;
copy in=exam out=finalexam;

select questionset1;

quit;

200: Explain the significance of EXCLUDE statement while using COPY statement.

Answer:

EXCLUDE statement is used with COPY statement when you want to copy an entire library except few datasets.

E.g.: The following program starts the dataset procedure and specifies the input library to be 'exam'. COPY statement specifies the name of the name of the library from which files are copied in the IN= option and specifies the name of the library to which the files are to be copied in OUT= option. EXCLUDE statement specifies the name of the dataset which needs to be excluded. Here all the files except dataset questionset1 is to be copied from 'exam' library to 'finalexam' library.

proc datasets;

copy in=exam out=finalexam;

exclude questionset1;

quit;

HR Questions

Review these typical interview questions and think about how you would answer them. Read the answers listed; you will find best possible answers along with strategies and suggestions.

1: Where do you find ideas?
Answer:
Ideas can come from all places, and an interviewer wants to see that your ideas are just as varied. Mention multiple places that you gain ideas from, or settings in which you find yourself brainstorming. Additionally, elaborate on how you record ideas or expand upon them later.

2: How do you achieve creativity in the workplace?
Answer:
It's important to show the interviewer that you're capable of being resourceful and innovative in the workplace, without stepping outside the lines of company values. Explain where ideas normally stem from for you (examples may include an exercise such as list-making or a mind map), and connect this to a particular task in your job that it would be helpful to be creative in.

3: How do you push others to create ideas?
Answer:
If you're in a supervisory position, this may be requiring employees to submit a particular number of ideas, or to complete regular idea-generating exercises, in order to work their creative muscles. However, you can also push others around you to create ideas simply by creating more of your own. Additionally, discuss with the interviewer the importance of questioning people as a way to inspire ideas and change.

4: Describe your creativity.

Answer:

Try to keep this answer within the professional realm, but if you have an impressive background in something creative outside of your employment history, don't be afraid to include it in your answer also. The best answers about creativity will relate problem-solving skills, goal-setting, and finding innovative ways to tackle a project or make a sale in the workplace. However, passions outside of the office are great, too (so long as they don't cut into your work time or mental space).

5: Would you rather receive more authority or more responsibility at work?

Answer:

There are pros and cons to each of these options, and your interviewer will be more interested to see that you can provide a critical answer to the question. Receiving more authority may mean greater decision-making power and may be great for those with outstanding leadership skills, while greater responsibility may be a growth opportunity for those looking to advance steadily throughout their careers.

6: What do you do when someone in a group isn't contributing their fair share?

Answer:

This is a particularly important question if you're interviewing for a position in a supervisory role – explain the ways in which you would identify the problem, and how you would go about pulling aside the individual to discuss their contributions. It's important to understand the process of creating a dialogue, so that you can communicate your expectations clearly to the individual, give them a chance to respond, and to make clear what needs to change. After this, create an action plan with the group member to ensure their contributions are on par with others in the group.

7: Tell me about a time when you made a decision that was outside of your authority.
Answer:
While an answer to this question may portray you as being decisive and confident, it could also identify you to an employer as a potential problem employee. Instead, it may be best to slightly refocus the question into an example of a time that you took on additional responsibilities, and thus had to make decisions that were outside of your normal authority (but which had been granted to you in the specific instance). Discuss how the weight of the decision affected your decision-making process, and the outcomes of the situation.

8: Are you comfortable going to supervisors with disputes?
Answer:
If a problem arises, employers want to know that you will handle it in a timely and appropriate manner. Emphasize that you've rarely had disputes with supervisors in the past, but if a situation were to arise, you feel perfectly comfortable in

discussing it with the person in question in order to find a resolution that is satisfactory to both parties.

9: If you had been in charge at your last job, what would you have done differently?
Answer:
No matter how many ideas you have about how things could run better, or opinions on the management at your previous job, remain positive when answering this question. It's okay to show thoughtful reflection on how something could be handled in order to increase efficiency or improve sales, but be sure to keep all of your suggestions focused on making things better, rather than talking about ways to eliminate waste or negativity.

10: Do you believe employers should praise or reward employees for a job well done?
Answer:
Recognition is always great after completing a difficult job, but there are many employers who may ask this question as a way to infer as to whether or not you'll be a high-maintenance worker. While you may appreciate rewards or praise, it's important to convey to the interviewer that you don't require accolades to be confident that you've done your job well. If you are interviewing for a supervisory position where you would be the one praising other employees, highlight the importance of praise in boosting team morale.

11: What do you believe is the most important quality a leader can have?

Answer:

There are many important skills for a leader to have in any business, and the most important component of this question is that you explain why the quality you choose to highlight is important. Try to choose a quality such as communication skills, or an ability to inspire people, and relate it to a specific instance in which you displayed the quality among a team of people.

12: Tell me about a time when an unforeseen problem arose. How did you handle it?

Answer:

It's important that you are resourceful, and level-headed under pressure. An interviewer wants to see that you handle problems systematically, and that you can deal with change in an orderly process. Outline the situation clearly, including all solutions and results of the process you implemented.

13: Can you give me an example of a time when you were able to improve *X objective* at your previous job?

Answer:

It's important here to focus on an improvement you made that created tangible results for your company. Increasing efficiency is certainly a very important element in business, but employers are also looking for concrete results such as increased sales or cut expenses. Explain your process thoroughly, offering specific numbers and evidence wherever possible, particularly in outlining the results.

14: Tell me about a time when a supervisor did not provide specific enough direction on a project.
Answer:
While many employers want their employees to follow very specific guidelines without much decision-making power, it's important also to be able to pick up a project with vague direction and to perform self-sufficiently. Give examples of necessary questions that you asked, and specify how you determined whether a question was something you needed to ask of a supervisor or whether it was something you could determine on your own.

15: Tell me about a time when you were in charge of leading a project.
Answer:
Lead the interviewer through the process of the project, just as you would have with any of your team members. Explain the goal of the project, the necessary steps, and how you delegated tasks to your team. Include the results, and what you learned as a result of the leadership opportunity.

16: Tell me about a suggestion you made to a former employer that was later implemented.
Answer:
Employers want to see that you're interested in improving your

company and doing your part – offer a specific example of something you did to create a positive change in your previous job. Explain how you thought of the idea, how your supervisors received it, and what other employees thought was the idea was put into place.

17: Tell me about a time when you thought of a way something in the workplace could be done more efficiently.
Answer:
Focus on the positive aspects of your idea. It's important not to portray your old company or boss negatively, so don't elaborate on how inefficient a particular system was. Rather, explain a situation in which you saw an opportunity to increase productivity or to streamline a process, and explain in a general step-by-step how you implemented a better system.

18: Is there a difference between leading and managing people – which is your greater strength?
Answer:
There is a difference – leaders are often great idea people, passionate, charismatic, and with the ability to organize and inspire others, while managers are those who ensure a system runs, facilitate its operations, make authoritative decisions, and who take great responsibility for all aspects from overall success to the finest decisions. Consider which of these is most applicable to the position, and explain how you fit into this role, offering concrete examples of your past experience.

19: Do you function better in a leadership role, or as a worker on a team?
Answer:
It is important to consider what qualities the interviewer is looking for in your position, and to express how you embody this role. If you're a leader, highlight your great ideas, drive and passion, and ability to incite others around you to action. If you work great in teams, focus on your dedication to the task at hand, your cooperation and communication skills, and your ability to keep things running smoothly.

20: Tell me about a time when you discovered something in the workplace that was disrupting your (or others) productivity – what did you do about it?
Answer:
Try to not focus on negative aspects of your previous job too much, but instead choose an instance in which you found a positive, and quick, solution to increase productivity. Focus on the way you noticed the opportunity, how you presented a solution to your supervisor, and then how the change was implemented (most importantly, talk about how you led the change initiative). This is a great opportunity for you to display your problem-solving skills, as well as your resourceful nature and leadership skills.

21: How do you perform in a job with clearly-defined objectives and goals?
Answer:

It is important to consider the position when answering this question – clearly, it is best if you can excel in a job with clearly-defined objectives and goals (particularly if you're in an entry level or sales position). However, if you're applying for a position with a leadership role or creative aspect to it, be sure to focus on the ways that you additionally enjoy the challenges of developing and implementing your own ideas.

22: How do you perform in a job where you have great decision-making power?

Answer:

The interviewer wants to know that, if hired, you won't be the type of employee who needs constant supervision or who asks for advice, authority, or feedback every step of the way. Explain that you work well in a decisive, productive environment, and that you look forward to taking initiative in your position.

23: If you saw another employee doing something dishonest or unethical, what would you do?

Answer:

In the case of witnessing another employee doing something dishonest, it is always best to act in accordance with company policies for such a situation – and if you don't know what this company's specific policies are, feel free to simply state that you would handle it according to the policy and by reporting it to the appropriate persons in charge. If you are aware of the company's policies (such as if you are seeking a promotion within your own company), it is best to specifically outline your actions according to the policy.

24: Tell me about a time when you learned something on your own that later helped in your professional life.
Answer:
This question is important because it allows the interviewer to gain insight into your dedication to learning and advancement. Choose an example solely from your personal life, and provide a brief anecdote ending in the lesson you learned. Then, explain in a clear and thorough manner how this lesson has translated into a usable skill or practice in your position.

25: Tell me about a time when you developed a project idea at work.
Answer:
Choose a project idea that you developed that was typical of projects you might complete in the new position. Outline where your idea came from, the type of research you did to ensure its success and relevancy, steps that were included in the project, and the end results. Offer specific before and after statistics, to show its success.

26: Tell me about a time when you took a risk on a project.
Answer:
Whether the risk involved something as complex as taking on a major project with limited resources or time, or simply volunteering for a task that was outside your field of

experience, show that you are willing to stretch out of your comfort zone and to try new things. Offer specific examples of why something you did was risky, and explain what you learned in the process – or how this prepared you for a job objective you later faced in your career.

27: What would you tell someone who was looking to get into this field?
Answer:
This question allows you to be the expert – and will show the interviewer that you have the knowledge and experience to go along with any training and education on your resume. Offer your knowledge as advice of unexpected things that someone entering the field may encounter, and be sure to end with positive advice such as the passion or dedication to the work that is required to truly succeed.

28: Tell me about a time when you didn't meet a deadline.
Answer:
Ideally, this hasn't happened – but if it has, make sure you use a minor example to illustrate the situation, emphasize how long ago it happened, and be sure that you did as much as you could to ensure that the deadline was met. Additionally, be sure to include what you learned about managing time better or prioritizing tasks in order to meet all future deadlines.

29: How do you eliminate distractions while working?
Answer:

With the increase of technology and the ease of communication, new distractions arise every day. Your interviewer will want to see that you are still able to focus on work, and that your productivity has not been affected, by an example showing a routine you employ in order to stay on task.

30: Tell me about a time when you worked in a position with a weekly or monthly quota to meet. How often were you successful?

Answer:

Your numbers will speak for themselves, and you must answer this question honestly. If you were regularly met your quotas, be sure to highlight this in a confident manner and don't be shy in pointing out your strengths in this area. If your statistics are less than stellar, try to point out trends in which they increased toward the end of your employment, and show reflection as to ways you can improve in the future.

31: Tell me about a time when you met a tough deadline, and how you were able to complete it.

Answer:

Explain how you were able to prioritize tasks, or to delegate portions of an assignments to other team members, in order to deal with a tough deadline. It may be beneficial to specify why the deadline was tough – make sure it's clear that it was not a result of procrastination on your part. Finally, explain how you were able to successfully meet the deadline, and what it took to get there in the end.

32: How do you stay organized when you have multiple projects on your plate?

Answer:

The interviewer will be looking to see that you can manage your time and work well – and being able to handle multiple projects at once, and still giving each the attention it deserves, is a great mark of a worker's competence and efficiency. Go through a typical process of goal-setting and prioritizing, and explain the steps of these to the interviewer, so he or she can see how well you manage time.

33: How much time during your work day do you spend on "auto-pilot?"

Answer:

While you may wonder if the employer is looking to see how efficient you are with this question (for example, so good at your job that you don't have to think about it), but in almost every case, the employer wants to see that you're constantly thinking, analyzing, and processing what's going on in the workplace. Even if things are running smoothly, there's usually an opportunity somewhere to make things more efficient or to increase sales or productivity. Stress your dedication to ongoing development, and convey that being on "auto-pilot" is not conducive to that type of success.

34: How do you handle deadlines?

Answer:

The most important part of handling tough deadlines is to prioritize tasks and set goals for completion, as well as to delegate or eliminate unnecessary work. Lead the interviewer through a general scenario, and display your competency through your ability to organize and set priorities, and most importantly, remain calm.

35: Tell me about your personal problem-solving process.
Answer:

Your personal problem-solving process should include outlining the problem, coming up with possible ways to fix the problem, and setting a clear action plan that leads to resolution. Keep your answer brief and organized, and explain the steps in a concise, calm manner that shows you are level-headed even under stress.

36: What sort of things at work can make you stressed?
Answer:

As it's best to stay away from negatives, keep this answer brief and simple. While answering that nothing at work makes you stressed will not be very believable to the interviewer, keep your answer to one generic principle such as when members of a team don't keep their commitments, and then focus on a solution you generally employ to tackle that stress, such as having weekly status meetings or intermittent deadlines along the course of a project.

37: What do you look like when you are stressed about something? How do you solve it?

Answer:

This is a trick question – your interviewer wants to hear that you don't look any different when you're stressed, and that you don't allow negative emotions to interfere with your productivity. As far as how you solve your stress, it's best if you have a simple solution mastered, such as simply taking deep breaths and counting to 10 to bring yourself back to the task at hand.

38: Can you multi-task?

Answer:

Some people can, and some people can't. The most important part of multi-tasking is to keep a clear head at all times about what needs to be done, and what priority each task falls under. Explain how you evaluate tasks to determine priority, and how you manage your time in order to ensure that all are completed efficiently.

39: How many hours per week do you work?

Answer:

Many people get tricked by this question, thinking that answering more hours is better – however, this may cause an employer to wonder why you have to work so many hours in order to get the work done that other people can do in a shorter amount of time. Give a fair estimate of hours that it should take you to complete a job, and explain that you are also willing to work extra whenever needed.

40: How many times per day do you check your email?
Answer:
While an employer wants to see that you are plugged into modern technology, it is also important that the number of times you check your email per day is relatively low – perhaps two to three times per day (dependent on the specific field you're in). Checking email is often a great distraction in the workplace, and while it is important to remain connected, much correspondence can simply be handled together in the morning and afternoon.

41: Describe a time when you communicated a difficult or complicated idea to a coworker.
Answer:
Start by explaining the idea briefly to the interviewer, and then give an overview of why it was necessary to break it down further to the coworker. Finally, explain the idea in succinct steps, so the interviewer can see your communication abilities and skill in simplification.

42: What situations do you find it difficult to communicate in?
Answer:
Even great communicators will often find particular situations that are more difficult to communicate effectively in, so don't be afraid to answer this question honestly. Be sure to explain

why the particular situation you name is difficult for you, and try to choose an uncommon answer such as language barrier or in time of hardship, rather than a situation such as speaking to someone of higher authority.

43: What are the key components of good communication?
Answer:
Some of the components of good communication include an environment that is free from distractions, feedback from the listener, and revision or clarification from the speaker when necessary. Refer to basic communication models where necessary, and offer to go through a role-play sample with the interviewer in order to show your skills.

44: Tell me about a time when you solved a problem through communication?
Answer:
Solving problems through communication is key in the business world, so choose a specific situation from your previous job in which you navigated a messy situation by communicating effectively through the conflict. Explain the basis of the situation, as well as the communication steps you took, and end with a discussion of why communicating through the problem was so important to its resolution.

45: Tell me about a time when you had a dispute with another employee. How did you resolve the situation?
Answer:

Make sure to use a specific instance, and explain step-by-step the scenario, what you did to handle it, and how it was finally resolved. The middle step, how you handled the dispute, is clearly the most definitive – describe the types of communication you used, and how you used compromise to reach a decision. Conflict resolution is an important skill for any employee to have, and is one that interviewers will search for to determine both how likely you are to be involved in disputes, and how likely they are to be forced to become involved in the dispute if one arises.

46: Do you build relationships quickly with people, or take more time to get to know them?
Answer:
Either of these options can display good qualities, so determine which style is more applicable to you. Emphasize the steps you take in relationship-building over the particular style, and summarize briefly why this works best for you.

47: Describe a time when you had to work through office politics to solve a problem.
Answer:
Try to focus on the positives in this question, so that you can use the situation to your advantage. Don't portray your previous employer negatively, and instead use a minimal instance (such as paperwork or a single individual), to highlight how you worked through a specific instance resourcefully. Give examples of communication skills or

problem-solving you used in order to achieve a resolution.

48: Tell me about a time when you persuaded others to take on a difficult task?
Answer:
This question is an opportunity to highlight both your leadership and communication skills. While the specific situation itself is important to offer as background, focus on how you were able to persuade the others, and what tactics worked the best.

49: Tell me about a time when you successfully persuaded a group to accept your proposal.
Answer:
This question is designed to determine your resourcefulness and your communication skills. Explain the ways in which you took into account different perspectives within the group, and created a presentation that would be appealing and convincing to all members. Additionally, you can pump up the proposal itself by offering details about it that show how well-executed it was.

50: Tell me about a time when you had a problem with another person, that, in hindsight, you wished you had handled differently.
Answer:
The key to this question is to show your capabilities of reflection and your learning process. Explain the situation,

how you handled it at the time, what the outcome of the situation was, and finally, how you would handle it now. Most importantly, tell the interviewer why you would handle it differently now – did your previous solution create stress on the relationship with the other person, or do you wish that you had stood up more for what you wanted? While you shouldn't elaborate on how poorly you handled the situation before, the most important thing is to show that you've grown and reached a deeper level of understanding as a result of the conflict.

51: Tell me about a time when you negotiated a conflict between other employees.
Answer:
An especially important question for those interviewing for a supervisory role – begin with a specific situation, and explain how you communicated effectively to each individual. For example, did you introduce a compromise? Did you make an executive decision? Or, did you perform as a mediator and encourage the employees to reach a conclusion on their own?

And Finally Good Luck!

INDEX

Base SAS Interview Questions

Basics

1: You might be already familiar with the dataset. What is the descriptor portion of the data set?
2: Which parameters describe a variable in SAS?
3: How does SAS recognise the end of a step and execute the previous step?
4: How do we reference a permanent SAS data set?
5: What is the default length of numeric variables?

Referencing Files

6: How do you verify after assigning a libref?
7: What is the purpose of a SAS engine?
8: Describe some ways to view the contents of SAS data set.
9: Which option is used to list the variables in creation order or order of logical position while viewing the dataset with proc contents?
10: How do you modify SAS system options like page number, time etc?
11: How SAS handles two digit year values?
12: Suppose your dataset exam.questionset2 contains 20 observations. How do you print only the last 11 observations?
13: Suppose your dataset exam.questionset2 contains 20 observations. How do you print the observations from 12-17?

14: Describe the SOURCE system option used in SAS?

15: Describe the REPLACE option in detail.

SAS Programs

16: What is the function of INCLUDE command in SAS?

17: What are the two categories of error commonly encountered in SAS?

18: Suppose after submitting a SAS program you see the statement 'Data step running' at the top of active window. What does that indicate and how do you resolve the issue?

19: How do you specify comments in SAS?

20: How do you invoke the debugger in SAS?

Reports – List and Summary

21: How do you select the variables and control the order in which they appear while creating a list report?

22: How to remove the column containing observation number while creating a list report?

23: What is the output of proc print?

24: How do you cancel a title statement?

25: Suppose you are having a data set exam.questionset2. The data set contains a column date. You have to assign a format (mmddyy8.) temporarily to the date column so that it appears in the formatted way in the output. How do you do that?

26: How do you assign a permanent label in SAS?

27: While creating a list report with proc report how do you select the variables and order them?

28: Which option is used with proc report statement to

underline all column headings and space between them?

29: What is the purpose of using order option in the define statement while using proc report?

30: Which variables are used to calculate statistics in proc report?

SAS Data Sets

31: What is the function of infile statement?

32: Which is the ideal situation for using column input?

33: How do you read the data lines entered directly into the program?

34: What is the purpose of using the keyword _null_ in the data statement?

35: What is the purpose of PUT statement?

36: Which parameters are to be mentioned in the input statement while using column input?

37: Usage of programming statement is one common way of creating a SAS data set from raw data file. What is the other way of creating SAS data set from raw data file?

38: What is the scope of a filename statement?

39: What is the significance of SET statement in SAS?

40: Is it possible to use date constants to assign dates in ASSIGNMENT statements?

Data Step

41: Explain the compilation phase of data step in detail.

42: When is an input buffer created?

43: Explain the automatic variable _ERROR_.

44: Explain the significance of _N_.
45: How do you limit the number of observations that are read during the data step?

Formats

46: What is the maximum length of label?
47: Explain the function of the keyword FMTLIB.
48: How is VALUE statement used to create formats?
49: Which keyword is used in the value statement to label the missing value?

Statistics

50: Which is the ideal procedure to use for calculating the statistics for continuous numeric variables?
51: What are the default statistics produced by the MEANS procedure?
52: Suppose you had a dataset exam.set1 for which you wish to calculate the median of all numeric variables. How do you use the programming statements?
53: Which option is used in the PROC MEANS statement to limit the number of decimal places?
54: How do you specify variables in PROC MEANS statement?
55: Which statistics are generated for class variables in means procedure?
56: How can you prevent the default report creation in PROC MEANS?
57: What is the default output produced by PROC FREQ?
58: How do you specify variables to be processed by PROC

FREQ?

59: Explain the significance of NOCUM option.

60: What are the criteria for the data to be used for BY group processing?

61: What is the difference between the default output produced by PROC MEANS and PROC SUMMARY?

62: What are the default values produced when PROC FREQ is used for producing crosstabulations?

63: Which keyword is used with PROC MEANS to compute standard deviation?

64: How will you produce a report with PROC SUMMARY?

65: Which types of values are ideal for frequency distribution?

Outputs

66: Could you list some ODS destinations which are currently supported?

67: How do you use the ODS statement to open LISTING destination?

68: Which ODS destination is open by default?

69: Which keyword is used in ODS statements to close all the open destination at once?

70: How does ODS handle the output?

71: How do you write the ODS statements to create a simple HTML output?

72: Which option is used in ODS HTML statement to specify the location of storing the output?

Variables

73: How does the SUM statement deal with the missing values?

74: How does an ASSIGNMENT statement deal with the missing values?

75: How do you change the initial value of sum variable?

76: How do you consider the value of zero in SAS while using Boolean expressions?

77: While creating a new character variable in the assignment statement, how is the length of the variable determined?

78: Is it possible to assign length to a character variable created using assignment statement?

79: What is the function of KEEP= option?

80: HOW is DROP statement used in SAS PROCEDURE?

81: Which form of the DO statement checks the condition before each iteration of DO loop?

82: What is the result of the following IF statement?

83: Suppose you have a data set in which the variables are assigned with permanent labels. But you are submitting a proc step in which you are assigning a new label to one of the variables. What will be the displayed as the label for the variable- new one or the one which is permanently stored?

Combining Data Sets

84: How do you read a data set questionset1 which is stored in the library exam?

85: You might be aware of the DROP= option. What criteria should you use to decide whether to place the option in the set statement or data statement?

86: Which variables are created automatically when you are using BY statement with the SET statement?

87: How do you go straight to an observation in a data set without considering preceding observations?

88: What happens if we specify invalid values for point= variables?

89: How do you detect an end of data set while reading data?

90: Which conditions have to be checked while using point= option?

91: While performing one–to-one reading does the resulting data set contain all the observations and variables from the input data sets?

92: What is the maximum number of data sets which can be given as an input for APPEND procedure?

93: How does concatenating combine the input data sets?

94: What is the prerequisite for two data sets to be merged by MERGE statement?

95: How do you use the RENAME data set option?

96: How many variables can be renamed at one time using RENAME= option?

97: How does one-to-one merging produce output?

98: What is the functionality of IN= data set option?

99: What is the difference between PROC APPEND and concatenate?

100: In which scenarios do you prefer to use the data set option KEEP= rather than using the data set option DROP=?

SAS Functions

101: Which function is used to convert character data values to numeric data values?

102: How does SAS store a date value?

103: Explain the significance of the function MDY.

104: What is the significance of DATE function?

105: Which function can be used interchangeably with DATE function?

106: Name some functions which provide results which are analogous to the results produced by any SAS procedure like proc means.

107: What is a target variable?

108: What happens when a character value is used in arithmetic operations?

109: Is the automatic conversion of character value to numeric and vice versa permissible in WHERE statements?

110: Which function is used to extract the quarter of the year in which a given date is falling?

111: Explain the significance of WEEKDAY function.

112: Explain INTCK function in detail.

113: Which function is used to extract an integer value from a given numeric value?

114: What happens when you specify an invalid date as an argument in mdy function?

115: Explain INTNX function in detail.

116: What is the functionality of TRIM function?

117: Which function converts all the letters of a character expression to uppercase?

118: Is TRANWRD a character function? Explain the functionality.

119: Which function enables you to search any string within a character variable?

120: Name one function which is used to concatenate the strings in SAS.

121: What is the functionality of SCAN function?

122: Explain the significance of PROPCASE function.

123: What is the output of DAY function in SAS?

124: What is the default length which SCAN function assigns to the target variable?

125: Explain functionality of SUBSTR function.

DO Loops

126: How do you construct a basic DO loop in SAS or explain the syntax of DO loop.

127: What is the default increment value in DO loop?

128: Can DO loops be used to combine DATA and PROC steps?

129: In SAS is it allowed to decrement DO loop?

130: While specifying the number of iterations in DO loop in SAS, is it possible to list the items in series?

131: Which condition has to be taken care of while specifying variable names to specify the number of iterations in DO loop?

132: How does a DO UNTIL loop execute in SAS?

133: Explain the DO WHILE statement.

134: How do you create observation for each iteration of a DO loop?

135: Is it possible to nest DO loops in SAS?

Arrays

136: What is the scope of an array in SAS?

137: What will happen if you name an array with a function name?

138: In SAS is it possible to use array names in DROP, KEEP, LENGTH and FORMAT statements?

139: How do you define a one dimensional array?

140: How do you indicate the dimension of a one dimensional array?

141: Which term do you use to specify that the array includes all the numeric variables which are defined in the current data step?

142: Which function is used to determine number of elements in an array?

143: How do you define an array of character variables in SAS?

144: How do you assign initial values to the array element?

145: How do you define a two-dimensional array?

Raw Data

146: Define nonstandard numeric data.

147: What is free format data?

148: Which features of column input allow it to be used for reading raw data?

149: Which are the two input styles which SAS uses for reading data in fixed fields?

150: Which parameters are to be mentioned in the input

statement while using formatted input?

151: Which numeric informat can be used if the data contains commas, percentage signs, dashes and dollars?

152: What is fixed length record format?

153: Describe the significance of PAD option.

154: Which parameters are to be mentioned in the input statement while using list input?

155: Explain the significance of DLM= option.

156: Is it possible to specify a range of character variables in the input statement, if the values are sequential?

157: What are the main limitations of LIST input?

158: Which option enables you to read the missing values at the end of the record?

159: Which option is specified to read the missing values at the beginning or middle of the record?

160: How does the DSD option affect the way SAS treats delimiters when used with list input?

161: What happens when list input is used to read character variables whose value has length more than 8?

162: Which modifier is used with list input to read the character values having embedded blanks?

163: Which modifier is used along with list input to read the nonstandard data values?

164: How does an informat function when used with formatted input?

165: How does an informat function when used with modified list input?

166: What all parameters must be mentioned while using PUT

statement with LIST output?

167: Is it allowed to mix three types of input styles to read the raw data?

168: How do you use a PUT statement to write a character string to a raw data file?

169: Is it possible to skip certain fields while using list input?

Date and Time Value

170: While storing dates, does SAS make adjustments for daylight saving time?

171: Explain DATEw informat in detail.

172: What is the minimum acceptable field width for TIMEw. informat?

173: Explain WORDDATEw. format.

174: How does YEARCUTOFF= option affect the four digit year values?

175: Explain WEEKDATEw. format.

176: Explain TIMEw. informat.

177: How does SAS store date and time and what is the advantage?

Line Pointer Controls

178: Explain #n line pointer control in SAS.

179: Explain forward slash(/) line pointer control in SAS.

180: Is it possible to combine both the line pointer controls (#n and /) in a SAS program to read the data both sequentially and non-sequentially?

181: While reading a file which contains multiple records per observation, what all things need to be considered?

182: Explain the significance of REMOVE statement

183: Explain the trailing (@) line hold specifier.

184: Explain double trailing (@@) sign in detail.

185: When is a record which is held by double trailing (@@) line hold specifier released?

186: In which situations is double trailing (@@) not allowed?

187: When is a record which is held by single trailing (@) line hold specifier released?

188: Consider the situation where a record is held by a single trailing (@) sign and another input statement which has an (@) executes?

189: How do you deal with records with varying number of fields while using single trailing sign(@)?

190: Explain STOPOVER option in detail.

191: While reading the data from an external file, which option is used to determine the end of the file condition?

192: Explain FLOWOVER option in detail.

193: Explain TRUNCOVER option in detail.

194: Explain the LINESIZE option.

195: Is it possible to create more than one data set in a single data step?

196: How do you rename one or more data sets in the same library?

197: How do you modify a label which was permanently assigned in a data step previously?

198: Is it possible to rename variables in a dataset using data sets procedure?

199: Is it possible to copy the data sets from one library to another using programming statements?

200: Explain the significance of EXCLUDE statement while using COPY statement.

HR Questions

1: Where do you find ideas?

2: How do you achieve creativity in the workplace?

3: How do you push others to create ideas?

4: Describe your creativity.

5: Would you rather receive more authority or more responsibility at work?

6: What do you do when someone in a group isn't contributing their fair share?

7: Tell me about a time when you made a decision that was outside of your authority.

8: Are you comfortable going to supervisors with disputes?

9: If you had been in charge at your last job, what would you have done differently?

10: Do you believe employers should praise or reward employees for a job well done?

11: What do you believe is the most important quality a leader can have?

12: Tell me about a time when an unforeseen problem arose. How did you handle it?

13: Can you give me an example of a time when you were able to improve X objective at your previous job?

14: Tell me about a time when a supervisor did not provide specific enough direction on a project.

15: Tell me about a time when you were in charge of leading a project.

16: Tell me about a suggestion you made to a former employer that was later implemented.

17: Tell me about a time when you thought of a way something in the workplace could be done more efficiently.

18: Is there a difference between leading and managing people – which is your greater strength?

19: Do you function better in a leadership role, or as a worker on a team?

20: Tell me about a time when you discovered something in the workplace that was disrupting your (or others) productivity – what did you do about it?

21: How do you perform in a job with clearly-defined objectives and goals?

22: How do you perform in a job where you have great decision-making power?

23: If you saw another employee doing something dishonest or unethical, what would you do?

24: Tell me about a time when you learned something on your own that later helped in your professional life.

25: Tell me about a time when you developed a project idea at work.

26: Tell me about a time when you took a risk on a project.

27: What would you tell someone who was looking to get into this field?

28: Tell me about a time when you didn't meet a deadline.

29: How do you eliminate distractions while working?

30: Tell me about a time when you worked in a position with a weekly or monthly quota to meet. How often were you successful?

31: Tell me about a time when you met a tough deadline, and

how you were able to complete it.

32: How do you stay organized when you have multiple projects on your plate?

33: How much time during your work day do you spend on "auto-pilot?"

34: How do you handle deadlines?

35: Tell me about your personal problem-solving process.

36: What sort of things at work can make you stressed?

37: What do you look like when you are stressed about something? How do you solve it?

38: Can you multi-task?

39: How many hours per week do you work?

40: How many times per day do you check your email?

41: Describe a time when you communicated a difficult or complicated idea to a coworker.

42: What situations do you find it difficult to communicate in?

43: What are the key components of good communication?

44: Tell me about a time when you solved a problem through communication?

45: Tell me about a time when you had a dispute with another employee. How did you resolve the situation?

46: Do you build relationships quickly with people, or take more time to get to know them?

47: Describe a time when you had to work through office politics to solve a problem.

48: Tell me about a time when you persuaded others to take on a difficult task?

49: Tell me about a time when you successfully persuaded a group to accept your proposal.

50: Tell me about a time when you had a problem with another person, that, in hindsight, you wished you had handled differently.

51: Tell me about a time when you negotiated a conflict between other employees.

Some of the following titles might also be handy:

1. .NET Interview Questions You'll Most Likely Be Asked
2. 200 Interview Questions You'll Most Likely Be Asked
3. Access VBA Programming Interview Questions You'll Most Likely Be Asked
4. Adobe ColdFusion Interview Questions You'll Most Likely Be Asked
5. Advanced JAVA Interview Questions You'll Most Likely Be Asked
6. AJAX Interview Questions You'll Most Likely Be Asked
7. Algorithms Interview Questions You'll Most Likely Be Asked
8. Android Development Interview Questions You'll Most Likely Be Asked
9. Ant & Maven Interview Questions You'll Most Likely Be Asked
10. Apache Web Server Interview Questions You'll Most Likely Be Asked
11. ASP.NET Interview Questions You'll Most Likely Be Asked
12. Automated Software Testing Interview Questions You'll Most Likely Be Asked
13. BEA WebLogic Server Interview Questions You'll Most Likely Be Asked
14. C & C++ Interview Questions You'll Most Likely Be Asked
15. C# Interview Questions You'll Most Likely Be Asked
16. C++ Internals Interview Questions You'll Most Likely Be Asked
17. CCNA Interview Questions You'll Most Likely Be Asked
18. Cloud Computing Interview Questions You'll Most Likely Be Asked
19. Computer Architecture Interview Questions You'll Most Likely Be Asked
20. Core JAVA Interview Questions You'll Most Likely Be Asked
21. Data Structures & Algorithms Interview Questions You'll Most Likely Be Asked
22. Data WareHousing Interview Questions You'll Most Likely Be Asked
23. EJB 3.0 Interview Questions You'll Most Likely Be Asked
24. Entity Framework Interview Questions You'll Most Likely Be Asked
25. Fedora & RHEL Interview Questions You'll Most Likely Be Asked
26. GNU Development Interview Questions You'll Most Likely Be Asked
27. Hibernate, Spring & Struts Interview Questions You'll Most Likely Be Asked
28. HTML, XHTML and CSS Interview Questions You'll Most Likely Be Asked
29. HTML5 Interview Questions You'll Most Likely Be Asked
30. IBM WebSphere Application Server Interview Questions You'll Most Likely Be Asked
31. iOS SDK Interview Questions You'll Most Likely Be Asked
32. Java / J2EE Design Patterns Interview Questions You'll Most Likely Be Asked
33. Java / J2EE Interview Questions You'll Most Likely Be Asked
34. Java Messaging Service Interview Questions You'll Most Likely Be Asked
35. JavaScript Interview Questions You'll Most Likely Be Asked
36. JavaServer Faces Interview Questions You'll Most Likely Be Asked
37. JDBC Interview Questions You'll Most Likely Be Asked
38. jQuery Interview Questions You'll Most Likely Be Asked
39. JSP-Servlet Interview Questions You'll Most Likely Be Asked
40. JUnit Interview Questions You'll Most Likely Be Asked
41. Linux Commands Interview Questions You'll Most Likely Be Asked

42. Linux Interview Questions You'll Most Likely Be Asked
43. Linux System Administrator Interview Questions You'll Most Likely Be Asked
44. Mac OS X Lion Interview Questions You'll Most Likely Be Asked
45. Mac OS X Snow Leopard Interview Questions You'll Most Likely Be Asked
46. Microsoft Access Interview Questions You'll Most Likely Be Asked
47. Microsoft Excel Interview Questions You'll Most Likely Be Asked
48. Microsoft Powerpoint Interview Questions You'll Most Likely Be Asked
49. Microsoft Word Interview Questions You'll Most Likely Be Asked
50. MySQL Interview Questions You'll Most Likely Be Asked
51. NetSuite Interview Questions You'll Most Likely Be Asked
52. Networking Interview Questions You'll Most Likely Be Asked
53. OOPS Interview Questions You'll Most Likely Be Asked
54. Oracle DBA Interview Questions You'll Most Likely Be Asked
55. Oracle E-Business Suite Interview Questions You'll Most Likely Be Asked
56. ORACLE PL/SQL Interview Questions You'll Most Likely Be Asked
57. Perl Interview Questions You'll Most Likely Be Asked
58. PHP Interview Questions You'll Most Likely Be Asked
59. PMP Interview Questions You'll Most Likely Be Asked
60. Python Interview Questions You'll Most Likely Be Asked
61. RESTful JAVA Web Services Interview Questions You'll Most Likely Be Asked
62. Ruby Interview Questions You'll Most Likely Be Asked
63. Ruby on Rails Interview Questions You'll Most Likely Be Asked
64. SAP ABAP Interview Questions You'll Most Likely Be Asked
65. Selenium Testing Tools Interview Questions You'll Most Likely Be Asked
66. Silverlight Interview Questions You'll Most Likely Be Asked
67. Software Repositories Interview Questions You'll Most Likely Be Asked
68. Software Testing Interview Questions You'll Most Likely Be Asked
69. SQL Server Interview Questions You'll Most Likely Be Asked
70. Tomcat Interview Questions You'll Most Likely Be Asked
71. UML Interview Questions You'll Most Likely Be Asked
72. Unix Interview Questions You'll Most Likely Be Asked
73. UNIX Shell Programming Interview Questions You'll Most Likely Be Asked
74. VB.NET Interview Questions You'll Most Likely Be Asked
75. XLXP, XSLT, XPATH, XFORMS & XQuery Interview Questions You'll Most Likely Be Asked
76. XML Interview Questions You'll Most Likely Be Asked
77. Base SAS Interview Questions You'll Most Likely Be Asked

For complete list visit
www.vibrantpublishers.com

NOTES

CPSIA information can be obtained at www.ICGtesting.com
Printed in the USA
BVOW06s0337130216

436600BV00015B/171/P